Late Adulthood:
Perspectives
on Human Development

Life-Span Human Development Series

Series Editors: Freda Rebelsky, Boston University, and Lynn Dorman

Infancy
Kathryn Sherrod, George Peabody College for Teachers
Peter Vietze, George Peabody College for Teachers
Steven Friedman, South Shore Mental Health Center

Early Childhood
Donald L. Peters, The Pennsylvania State University
Sherry L. Willis, The Pennsylvania State University

The Middle Years of Childhood
Patricia Minuchin, Temple University

Adolescence
Kathleen M. White, Boston University
Joseph C. Speisman, Boston University

Early and Middle Adulthood
Lillian E. Troll, Rutgers University

Late Adulthood: Perspectives on Human Development
Richard A. Kalish, Berkeley, California

Cross-Cultural Human Development
Robert L. Munroe, Pitzer College
Ruth H. Munroe, Pitzer College

Life-Span Developmental Psychology:
Introduction to Research Methods
Paul B. Baltes, The Pennsylvania State University
Hayne W. Reese, West Virginia University
John R. Nesselroade, The Pennsylvania State University

Biological Perspectives in Developmental Psychology
George F. Michel, Boston University
Celia L. Moore, University of Massachusetts

Late Adulthood: Perspectives on Human Development

Richard A. Kalish
Berkeley, California

BROOKS/COLE PUBLISHING COMPANY
MONTEREY, CALIFORNIA
A Division of Wadsworth Publishing Company, Inc.

This book is dedicated to the memory of my father, Max Kalish (1891–1945), and to the memories of Donald P. Kent (1916–1972), Margaret Blenkner (1909–1973), and Jennie Borak Goldfarb (1918–1973), none of whom were given the opportunity to know what it was like to grow old. Their lives and their deaths are incorporated in this book and in my life in many ways.

ISBN: 0-8185-0144-8
L.C. Catalog Card No.: 74-18923
Printed in the United States of America

10 9 8 7 6 5

Production Editor: *Lyle York*
Interior Design: *Linda Marcetti*
Cover Design: *John Edeen*
Typesetting: *Datagraphics Press, Inc., Phoenix, Arizona*
Printing & Binding: *Malloy Lithographing, Inc., Ann Arbor, Michigan*

Series Foreword

What are the changes we see over the life span? How can we explain them? And how do we account for individual differences? The Life-Span Human Development Series provides a new way to look at these questions. It approaches human development from three major perspectives: (1) a focus on basic issues related to the study of life-span developmental psychology, such as methodology and research design, cross-cultural and longitudinal studies, age-stage phenomena, and stability and change; (2) a focus on age divisions—infancy, early childhood, middle childhood, adolescence, young and middle adulthood, and late adulthood; and (3) a focus on developmental areas such as physiology, cognition, language, perception, sex roles, and personality.

There is some overlap in the content of these volumes. We believe that it will be stimulating to the reader to think the same idea through from the viewpoints of different authors or from the viewpoints of different areas of development. For example, language development is the subject of one volume and is also discussed in the volume on cross-cultural development, among others.

Instructors and students may use the entire series for a thorough survey of life-span developmental psychology or, since each volume can be used independently, may choose selected volumes to cover specific concept areas or age ranges. Volumes that focus on basic issues can be used to introduce the student to the life-span concept.

No single author could adequately cover the entire field as we have defined it. Our authors found it exciting to focus on their areas of specialization within a limited space while, at the same time, expanding their thinking to encompass the entire life span. It can be beneficial to both author and student to attempt a new integration of familiar material. Since we think it also benefits students to see ideas in development, we encouraged the authors not only to review the relevant literature but also to use what they now know to point up possible new areas of study. As a result, the student will learn to think about human development rather than just learn the facts of development.

Freda Rebelsky

Lynn Dorman

Preface

Growing older means getting wiser. Growing older means thinking about exercising regularly and quitting smoking. Getting older means remembering all the people who have meant something to you and all the different freaky things you've done. Getting older means looking forward to even more because you're starting to learn to get it on, even when you're scared to death. Getting older means learning to appreciate yourself. Having birthdays means wanting to have a party with your friends.

From an invitation to the joint birthday party of Maia Craig and Roberto Almanzon, as they became 30 and 36, respectively.

Growing older is a process experienced by everyone, and birthdays are reminders that this process is indeed ongoing. People in their twenties and thirties can draw very real insights from their own experiences into what it means to be aging. There is room for optimism and a little sadness, for the awareness that some behavior may change, for marshaling and utilizing your own resources, for reminiscing about the past, and for looking with hope into the future. Those who are not yet old have had ample experiences to gain some empathy for those who are.

Through this book, I hope to enable the not-yet-old to expand their understanding of aging and their empathy for the elderly by examining the issues, the ideas, and the information available on the psychology of later maturity and old age. In so doing, I have attempted to provide a realistic picture of older people, avoiding the temptation to gain sympathy for them by emphasizing their health and economic problems, their limitations, and their loneliness and lack of power, while simultaneously avoiding the pollyannaish notions that old age is a period of comfortable ease and pleasure, without important worries or cares.

There are several audiences for whom this book was written. First, I believe it would fit in well with the final weeks of a life-span development course. Second, in combination with a good book of readings or with a well-designed reading list, it would serve as the basic text for a full course on aging. Third, there are many continuing-education programs, workshops, and seminars on human aging that might find this book useful. Fourth, students who wonder whether they wish to probe deeper into the psychology of aging could begin by reading or even skimming this book. And fifth, I very much hope that nonstudents who are interested in the psychology of aging and the elderly themselves who wonder what the academics have to say about them would pick up this book to browse through.

I have made only one assumption about the background of persons reading this book: that they have had either one formal course in psychology or the equivalent amount of informal reading. I have used some basic concepts of psychology that are not always fully explained in the book, although most can be understood from the context.

Even though the book is essentially psychological and psychosocial, it has been written with the assumption that it may be useful to students in many fields and professions, such as social welfare, nursing, psychiatry, sociology, urban studies, education, public health, counseling, and recreation. And, although it is essentially a textbook, I would like to believe that it also has value for persons who are not enrolled in any class but who simply want to learn more about human aging.

This book is written primarily so that you can learn a little more about older people and what it means to age, but another kind of awareness is inevitable. Each of you will probably wonder about yourself as you grow older: Does this sentence apply to me? Will I suffer this loss, have this capacity reduced, become more of this or less of that? If so, will I cope successfully, or will I become lonely, depressed, unhappy? Speaking only for myself, I firmly believe that my own involvement in the field of aging has offered me more options as I get older, has helped me to understand some of the changes I see in myself as being anticipated and normal, and has permitted me greater perspective and even a touch of humor about getting old. I feel strongly that an awareness of the human aging process will enable each of us to cope much more effectively with the aging of those we love, with the aging of our friends and associates, and with the aging that will inevitably come to each of us.

As always, many people have participated in making this a better book than I possibly could have by myself. These are Jeanne Bader (University of California, San Francisco), Herman Brotman (private consultant, Washington, D. C., and Falls Church, Virginia), Ira B. Cross (retired from University of California, Berkeley, in 1952), Andrew Dibner (Boston University), Aronna Hubert (University of California, Los Angeles), M. Powell Lawton (Philadelphia Geriatric Center), Beatrice Schiffman (National Council on the Aging, San Francisco), Lillian Troll (Wayne State University), and three who typed and otherwise corrected the manuscript in various stages: Ann Johnson, Barbara Saito, and Deby Watson.

Richard A. Kalish

Contents

Chapter One

Human Aging: An Orientation

In the time that it took you to read the first 12 words of this sentence, you have aged: you have partaken of the universal phenomenon occurring to humans and lower animals, to animate and inanimate objects, to ideas and cultures. You have aged; you have changed; you have come one more step along the path to your own eventual demise. True—you may prefer to use the concept of "development" rather than the notion of "aging," since the one implies an unlimited future, whereas the other suggests, at least to many people, a decremental process. But the concept you prefer does not alter the fact: *you are aging.*

Aging is a process that is sometimes favorable and sometimes unfavorable, but it is—with our present state of knowledge—a natural and inevitable process. Being old, elderly, aged, a "senior citizen," a "golden ager," is a stage in this process, occurring just as naturally and just as inevitably (except, of course, for those who die earlier) as infancy and childhood. Neither the process of aging nor the state of being old is pathological, strange, or deviant except as the result of certain unpleasant occurrences that tend to be age-related, much as other unpleasant occurrences are associated with the preschool years or the middle years of life.

My purpose in this abrupt beginning is not to distress you or frighten you into or out of reading further. Rather, I wish to stress that human existence is a continuum with conception at one end and death at the other, and that the later years, even the terminal days, need to be seen as part of this continuum. Later life should be approached not as a social problem, although for many it is, but as the final stages of a span of development that is continuous with the earlier stages.

Like people of any age group, those in their later years share certain qualities, feelings, experiences, roles, and changes with their age cohorts;

but, like people of any age group, those in their later years are also immensely variable in their qualities, feelings, experiences, roles, and changes
and immensely different from others of their age group.

Why Study the Later Years?

"Old people are on their way out. We need to focus on those who
will be around awhile and can help build a better world."

"Getting old just isn't relevant for me. It's simply too far away."

"Old people are beyond change and beyond meaningful interventions. Their best years are behind them. Too much input for too little
output."

"Their values and ideas and habits are so different from mine that
I can't really deal with them."

"I just don't want to think about getting old and dying. It's too
depressing."

Yet anyone who is truly concerned with the dignity of all human
beings, who really wishes to understand humankind in its entirety, who
desires more than a segmentalized view of life, needs to understand the later
years. For me, there are three basic reasons to study the psychology of the
later years.

1. To participate in providing resources for those who are old
today and for those who will be old tomorrow (that is, you and me) so that
they—and we—lead a more satisfactory life during the later years

2. To enable us to better understand our own relationships to older
persons and to our own aging process so that we can lead a more satisfactory
life ourselves today

3. To place the earlier years of the life span in proper perspective
and to perceive individual development as a lifelong process

These reasons might be labeled service, insight, and theory. I will
attempt to provide a balance among these approaches in the coming pages.

Some Definitions

When is "old"?

As you might expect, there is no one correct answer to that question. Several different approaches are used, each justifiable and each open
to criticism. "Old" can be defined strictly in chronological terms: when a
person reaches his sixty-fifth birthday, he is old. There are legal and economic bases for this definition, supported by rules regarding mandatory

retirement, by income tax regulations, by Social Security requirements, and —to some degree—by popular consent.

But you could also define "old" in terms of physical changes. These might include changes in body posture, gait, facial features, hair color and hairline, voice, skin resiliency, general body contour, and ability to hear and see. Perhaps health is a part of your definition. You have a general physical image of "old," and the closer an individual approximates your image, the more likely you are to perceive that person as old.

Organic changes become translated into behavior, and you might think of "old" in terms of forgetfulness (most likely the result, at least in large part, of organic brain changes), slower reaction time, altered sleeping patterns, slower motor behavior, and so forth. Or perhaps you have thought of "old" as defined in terms of ideas, concepts, and reactions to others. Some common stereotypes of the elderly are that they are conservative, hostile to the younger generation, resistant to social change, and easily irritated.

"Old" can also be defined in terms of social roles. "Old" is when an individual is retired, in a convalescent facility, a grandparent. Again, this is too simplistic, since hundreds of thousands of people have retired from one job, with pension, before they are 50; younger people can be placed in convalescent facilities; and grandparents in their forties are hardly unusual. Conversely, 60-year-olds occasionally return to college to complete degrees begun four decades earlier; reports of men (but virtually never women) becoming parents in their sixties and beyond are unusual, but not unheard-of. Although the concept of social age or of being socially old is useful, it is hardly sufficient definition by itself.

So you might settle for self-report. "Old" is when the person himself says "I guess I'm old." That definition solves some problems and creates others, such as how to categorize the 67-year-old professor who remarked, just after he retired, "I no longer resent being referred to as 'middle-aged.'"

In practice, most of us shift our definitions of "old" to suit the situation, often without fully realizing what we are doing. We judge one person old because he behaves in ways we judge old, but we talk easily about "older Americans" to refer to all persons 65 and over. Perhaps the most important consideration is that both the speaker and the listener share the same definition at the same time.

What to call the old. Old, elderly, aged, aging, senior citizen, golden ager, senescent, older adult, older person, older American, retiree, 65 plus. All these words are adequate and accurate, although "senior citizen" and "golden ager" happen to affect me—and a lot of the elderly—in a negative fashion. There are gradations of meaning among the terms, and the term that seems most accurate to me and least likely to irritate others is, simply, "older person" or, sometimes, "older American."

Individual differences at work. By using the arbitrary definition of "old" based on chronological age—more specifically, based on being 65 or older—over 21 million (1974 data) residents of the United States are old, some 10% of the entire population; 8% of Canadians also fall into this age bracket. Therefore, generalizations about the entire group are hazardous. Essentially, when we say "Older persons are . . .," we are saying one of five things:

1. All older persons are . . .
2. Almost all older persons are . . .
3. Most older persons are . . .
4. Compared to other age groups, older persons are . . .
5. Relative to their younger days, older persons are . . .

We are encompassing an age group that spans 40 or more years, that ranges from excellent physical and emotional health to imminent death or severe psychosis, from extreme levels of intellectual and cultural awareness to extreme limitations in such awareness, from being actively employed to being actively (or passively) retired, and on and on.

Behavior and performance among a randomly selected group of 100 newborns are not highly variable. There will be some differences (such as in the frequency and duration of crying, the intensity of sucking, and amount of bodily movement), but highly accurate predictions can be made about newborns based only on knowing their age and that they are basically normal. As people become older, our ability to predict behavior simply from knowing a person's chronological age diminishes. For the middle-aged, predictions are quite difficult to make: some are already performing in ways we associate with old age, whereas others are behaving in ways we associate with adolescence. Knowing that an individual is 3 years old, we can make fairly accurate estimates regarding his ability to walk a mile, to fix dinner for himself, to read and understand a newspaper article, and to memorize a poem; similarly, our ability to predict for a 40-year-old is still relatively good. For someone known to be 75, however, the accuracy of the prediction is reduced substantially. In brief, older adults vary more in biological and behavioral functioning than do younger adults (Botwinick & Thompson, 1968).

We can make certain general statements about older persons. "Older people are much more likely to be hurt by falling than younger people." "Most older persons are not presently employed for income." "Learning a new psychomotor task takes an older person longer than it takes a younger person." "Older adults include a much higher proportion of widows or widowers than any other age group." "Most Americans and Canadians will be over age 65 when they die." But even the most casual look at the statistics responsible for these statements will bring the immediate realization that great variability exists within the population over age 65.

To some extent, we can sharpen our predictions by specifying a particular subgroup of elderly. Women are much more likely to be living without a spouse than men. Those over 80 are much more likely to reside in an extended-care facility than those under 75. Black Americans are less likely to be over age 65 when they die than white Americans or Asian Americans. The elderly with incomes below average for the age group are much more likely to have housing or transportation problems than the elderly with above-average income.

Even within the cruder classifications of age (for example, 60–69, 70–79), sex, ethnicity, health status, income, or marital status, other demographic distinctions can be made. True, most elderly blacks are poor, but some are not; it is vital to recognize simultaneously both the concept of "most" and the existence of variability, so that we don't fall into the trap of stereotyping all elderly blacks as poor or all elderly women as widows or all elderly couples as grandparents.

Senescence. The period of life during which additional years produce decrements in functional ability is termed *senescence.* A senescent person is *not* necessarily senile! The changes that do accompany aging need not be incapacitating or even moderately disturbing. Not only are individual differences in the onset of general senescence great, as discussed above, but intraindividual differences are also great. That is, one's body does not necessarily age in a unitary fashion; certain organs or systems may show decrement sooner than others. A man of 70 may, for instance, retain a perfectly smooth, unwrinkled face, a full head of black hair, and a heart performing like that of a man in his fifties—while his renal functioning may be like that of an 80-year-old.

Gerontology and geriatrics. Gerontology is the study of the elderly (literally, the study of old men, from the Greek word *geros*). Geriatrics is the system of treatment of the elderly. Although geriatrics initially referred solely to treatment for health problems, the term is now applied to other fields, such as social work and recreation.

Very few people refer to themselves simply as gerontologists, since the study of the elderly and the aging process is a subspecialty of many different fields. A biologist will study the aging process of tissues or of one-celled animals; a sociologist may study housing for the elderly; an anthropologist might focus on the role of the older person in a preliterate community or on the social structure of a retirement community; an educator is concerned with devising effective continuing-education programs for recent retirees and preretirees; an economist investigates the ways in which Social Security and pension programs lead to income redistribution among age groups; a criminologist may be interested in the kinds of crime committed by older persons, in alternatives to imprisonment, or in what those with a long career of crime do when they reach their later years. Sometimes a gross differentiation is made between social gerontology and biological gerontology, with all but the biologist among the specialists named above being categorized as social gerontologists,

The psychological gerontologist has his own areas of special interest, such as the changes with age in memory, perception, reaction time, or intellectual functioning. He may also be concerned with marital roles and family relationships, the psychological impact of retirement, the meaning of one's own death and the loss of others through death, the psychological consequences of various living arrangements, loneliness and companionship, the treatment of mental illness, or the psychological effects of the aging process on personality characteristics. In short, anything that a psychologist normally studies, limited only by its having some application to later life, can be part of gerontology.

Research Methods in Psychological Gerontology

Behavioral scientific research in psychological gerontology is conducted in the same fashion as behavioral research with other age groups. Methods used include controlled observations, controlled laboratory experiments, field research, participant-observer research, a variety of tests, epidemiological studies and other uses of census data and large-scale survey research, interviews and questionnaires, analyses of social and organizational structure, and so forth.

Although it shares basic methodological procedures with research on other age groups, research with persons in their later years entails some unique opportunities and some unique difficulties. This fact is particularly evident when we try to differentiate age changes, generational differences, and accidents of history.

In order to understand what happens between the ages of 55 and 75, for instance, we have two basic options. We can study a group of 55-year-olds and a group of 75-year-olds, note the significant differences between the two groups, and assume that these differences arose because one group lived longer than the other. *Or* we can begin to study a group of 55-year-olds and follow them up at regular intervals until they reach the age of 75, and assume that the changes taking place have resulted from having lived for 20 years. The former is termed *cross-sectional* research; the latter is known as *longitudinal* research. Both have important advantages; both have major pitfalls. (Readers wishing to probe into ways of integrating these two methods should read Schaie & Strother, 1968.)

The cross-sectional approach has some obvious benefits. It can be done fairly quickly: you don't need to wait 20 years to obtain meaningful data. For that reason, it is also much less expensive in time, effort, and money. Also, by being conducted in a brief time span, it is much less affected by the accidents of history. For example, a longitudinal study of changes in physical health and health needs of the elderly begun in 1963 would have immense difficulty in determining the impact of the initiation of Medicare in 1966. Increased rates of visits to physicians and hospitals between 1960 and 1970 might have resulted from the greater availability of low-cost medical services, from increased health problems, from better health education, or from all of these factors.

Longitudinal studies also suffer from attrition. In all age groups, a portion of those who begin as participants in longitudinal research drop out before the end of the study. Perhaps they leave the area; they may become bored with the project or irritated with the investigators; or their schedules might make it inconvenient for them to continue. In working with the elderly, an even more difficult problem occurs: attrition through illness and death. A separate problem arises when those who do become too ill to continue or who die during the project differ in some important way from those who remain. Assume that we wish to learn more about changes in immediate memory over a ten-year period, and we begin in 1970 with 30 persons born in 1905, 30 more born in 1900, and an additional 30 born in 1895. We then administer various memory tests over a ten-year period and, in 1980, we trace the individuals still alive back across the previous decade to see what has occurred. Many of those who were part of the original sample will have died, and this part of the sample will contain a disproportionately large number of those who had lower memory scores when initially tested (Riegel & Riegel, 1972). We also know that a drop-off in certain kinds of cognitive behavior may be predictive of a health condition that can lead to death. Therefore, those who remain at the end of ten years were probably quite different at the beginning of the project from those lost through illness or death.

We have, nonetheless, learned something about changes in memory over time. Because we began with different age cohorts, the investigation had a cross-sectional component (that is, we could compare 65-year-olds, 70-year-olds, and 75-year-olds in 1970 and at subsequent times), so we had an additional source of data. We were also able to compare the performance of those who were 70 in 1970 with the performance in 1975 of those who turned 70 in that year, in order to verify that the changes we have observed happen to 70-year-olds in general and not just to one age cohort. (The term *age cohort* refers to those persons born during the same general time period.)

In summary, longitudinal research does provide substantial advantages. We do not need to assume that the sample of 75-year-olds is comparable to the sample of 65-year-olds, but we are able to use each person as his own control; that is, we can study the changes over time for each person. In a cross-sectional study, we would normally find that 70-year-olds are more likely to hold traditional religious values than 50-year-olds. Is that difference the result of their having lived 20 years longer? Or is it that people born 70 years ago were brought up in a social climate that was more likely to encourage such beliefs than the social climate of those born 50 years ago? Or a bit of both? An effective longitudinal study of religious beliefs would provide a partial answer to this question. It would also offer data as to who (among the individuals within each group) became more religious, who became less religious, and who retained earlier views.

Both cross-sectional and longitudinal studies are influenced by attrition: those already dead or too ill to participate differ in systematic ways from those who do take part. Moreover, there is good reason to assume that persons volunteering to participate in research are more capable than those who do not volunteer, and that those who remain with a longitudinal project to its completion are more capable than those who drop out along the line (Schaie, Labouvie, & Barrett, 1973).

In the final analysis, it appears best to go ahead with both longitudinal research and cross-sectional research, recognizing in our interpretations of the findings the limitations and strengths of each approach.

The Meaning of Psychological Gerontological Research

Research is the only way to provide the answers to important questions. Research is dehumanizing, an invasion of privacy. Research is meaningless because each individual is unique. Research takes dollars away from much more important services. Research is necessary to progress. Each of these statements is familiar, is based to some degree on a valid notion, and is a gross oversimplification of the actual circumstances.

First, and perhaps foremost, research in psychological gerontology, like all research, serves a variety of purposes. I will discuss these under three major categories: (1) theory-building or basic research, (2) "understanding" research, and (3) action and evaluation research. These are not clean-cut, mutually exclusive categories. Rather, they describe differing purposes and, often, differing methodologies. Any one study, however, may combine all three in varying degrees.

Basic Research

The purpose of conducting basic research is to uncover principles of human aging and of the behavior and functioning of older people that can be generalized to other settings. Researchers hope that these principles will have applicability today and 30 years in the future, in North America and in Southeast Asia, in rural areas and in suburban areas. Although the person conducting basic research may be deeply and personally concerned about the human condition of the elderly, the practical application of his or her research is usually left to others.

One pair of investigators looked into the effects of practice on the short-term memory of young and old individuals. (Short-term memory involves recall within a few minutes or a couple of hours after the learning experience, as opposed to long-term memory, which represents recall after a period of weeks, months, or years.) The task was a simple one: to view a series of two-digit numbers and report orally the pair of numbers in proper sequence when asked very shortly afterward. Subjects took part in five such sessions, spread out over a month, to permit improvement from practice. The purpose was to determine whether older subjects would improve more from practice than younger subjects; it is reasonably well established that younger persons do better, on the average, on the task itself. The results indicated that, although the practice opportunity did not help older people more than younger people, both groups did improve their memory span as a result of the practice. (If you wish to read the study in detail, see Taub & Long, 1972.)

Another study, much broader in scope, investigated the extent to which the social relationships of older people were affected by the age distribution of residents of the apartment buildings in which they lived. Specifically, the investigator hypothesized that "the number of their local friends and the amount of their interaction with neighbors will be directly related to the residential concentration of the aged" (Rosow, 1967, p. 41). The findings clearly supported the idea that older persons fare better when they reside in apartments with a high proportion of other elderly, although specific exceptions were noted and discussed by the author.

Both projects were aimed at improving theories of the behavior of the elderly, the former concerned with theories of learning and forgetting and the latter with theories of social integration and relatedness. Both studies were planned and executed to provide for maximum generalizability to other segments of the elderly population. Neither investigation settled its questions for all time and all space, but the findings of both investigations could be applied far beyond the samples directly involved, especially when integrated with findings from other projects that probed similar considerations. Although these studies have direct implications for adult educators, community planners, adult children of elderly persons, and recent retirees contemplating their future housing needs, theoretical considerations were probably of higher priority to the investigators than these practical outcomes.

"Understanding" Research

Research that moves one step toward the applied, but that still has theoretical implications, is what I have termed "understanding" research. These studies are more limited to the space and time in which they are conducted; that is, they have more limited generalizability and are more affected by the specific situation in which they are conducted.

One such study investigated the food-shopping behavior of an elderly urban population in Denver, Colorado. The investigators interviewed 401 older persons outside a variety of food markets, asking them questions about how they got to the store, whether there were particular difficulties in getting there or getting home (there were, especially for those who walked: crossing major streets, carrying heavy sacks of groceries), and how much they spent. The results were closely related to the kind of market involved (a large supermarket in a shopping center or a small neighborhood store), how they arrived there (walking or driving), their income, and related matters (Sherman & Brittan, 1973). The authors discussed their results in terms of the significance of the increasing use of shopping centers and diminished availability of neighborhood stores. Although this study certainly has implications for other communities and other groups of elderly, and although it has some implications for theory, I consider its main strength to be that it is a carefully described case history helpful in the understanding of the elderly.

An anthropologist has written an article entitled "The Changing Status of Elders in a Polynesian Society" (Maxwell, 1970). Again, implications for theory were evident, but the primary value of the paper lies in the insights shed on aging in another culture, both in understanding that culture and its people and in pointing up, by means of contrast, what is taking place in our culture.

Action or Evaluation Research

Some gerontological research is applied directly to solving practical problems. Such research may be employed in the evaluation of a specific program or may try to come to grips with a policy or problem of immediate concern.

One very popular and successful project has been the Foster Grandparent program, which involves the utilization of older persons as grandparent surrogates for institutionalized children. Normally, the older participants live on a limited income and are paid a small amount for their work. The children may be mentally retarded, physically handicapped, emotionally disturbed, or simply living in an institutional setting because they lack access to an appropriate family arrangement.

Under most circumstances, a Foster Grandparent program would have several goals, including increasing the life satisfaction of the older participant, increasing the life satisfaction of the children, providing low-income elderly with additional money, and improving the services offered by the children's institution. It would be difficult to oppose such a program, but we can still ask some knotty questions. For example, are the children really better off for having spent a couple of hours a day five days a week with an older person? Conversely, does the experience really add to the life satisfaction of the older person? Moreover, what can we learn to help us select those older persons who will function most effectively? What is the best kind of training program for these people? What is the impact on the child when his foster grandparent stops coming, because of illness or death or through the elimination of program funding? How can the child be best compensated for this kind of loss? And a final and most practical question: could the same goals be better achieved in some other fashion, such as by using volunteers instead of paying the foster grandparents, or by dividing all available money equally among the older participants instead of covering the salaries of professional community organizers?

Some foster-grandparent arrangements have succeeded, while others have not. Therefore, our research might be directed not only at the program in its totality but also at specific locations, trying to untangle the factors that keep enthusiasm high in one community and lead to bickering and unhappiness in another.

Some of these issues were studied in a research program designed much along the lines described above. The foster grandparents in this instance showed a marked improvement in satisfaction, based not only on their increased income but also on their remaining active, having a "reason to get up in the morning," feeling healthy and vigorous, and gaining general self-esteem. Of the foster grandparents who dropped out of the program, the majority left for health reasons. Some of these did refer to difficulties arising from having become too attached to the children, but "almost all the former foster-grandparents expressed persistent feelings of pride associated with the experience" (Saltz, 1971, p. 330).

Innumerable opportunities for program evaluation exist. How effective are present health-care delivery systems? What is the impact on a healthy and alert older person of living in a high-rise apartment where only the elderly are permitted to reside? What is the outcome of a good nutrition program? The term *program evaluation* is normally applied when a specific project, such as a Foster Grandparent program in Reno, a geriatric day-care center in White Plains, New York, or a nutrition program in Miami, is evaluated. *Action research* is a term used primarily when the scope of the study is broader—for example, the evaluation of the Foster Grandparent program, geriatric day-care centers, or nutritional programs in general. The term *action research* also applies when a policy is being studied and the findings are to be used to improve a program or project.

Program Goals

In order to judge the success of a program or of any other form of intervention, we need to establish goals. Perhaps the first question to ask is: for whom has the program been set up? Normally you would assume that the desired outcome is greater life satisfaction for the older people involved, but more careful analysis of the situation might suggest that other goals may take precedence: for example, ensuring the smooth functioning of a hospital, easing political pressures, reducing financial costs, assuaging the anger or guilt of adult children, or several of these goals in concert.

Even when only the elderly are at issue, goals are not always clear. A conflict may arise between allocating resources to health care and allocating them toward encouraging human interactions, between the kinds of recreation the older participants request and the activities preferred by the professional staff, between keeping people in their home and community and giving them optimum institutional care. A well-designed program and a carefully planned evaluation can take all these matters into account, but the task is not a simple one.

A common programmatic goal, which evaluation research must reflect, is to enable the older participants to become more self-sufficient. This goal assumes that certain of the behavior patterns defined as "old" or as otherwise negative can be altered by the intervention. Anyone working with the elderly has seen this occur. An older woman who has been sitting in her living room watching television (or at least staring at the moving pattern of lights and darks on the screen) is referred to a geriatric day-care center, with the accompanying explanation that she rarely speaks, moves slowly and only when she must, and is believed to be following a downhill path. After a few sessions at the center, where she can talk with other older persons, participate in some form of physical activity, and obtain the individual attention of a student volunteer, the downhill path is shown to be reversible. Her cognitive performance improves; so do her appetite and her willingness to converse. Indeed, she seems to have regained some zest for living. So, in some instances, the perceived process of decrement as an apparent function of aging is reversible.

On other occasions, the downhill path cannot be reversed, but the person can continue for a considerable period of time without showing further decrement. And there are times when the only option available to the staff is to slow the downhill path or, in more extreme circumstances, to enable an older person who displays definite changes for the worse to gain greater satisfaction from the kinds of experiences in which he or she can still participate.

In working with children or nonelderly adults, program planners normally think in terms of permitting the individual to function as a socially and physically effective person, operating in a self-sufficient manner in the outside community. This is not always possible with the aged, especially with the very old, and other goals may be more important in planning programs and designing related evaluation research. However, geriatric workers and researchers may find it difficult to adjust to the limitations (or at least the possible limitations, since you are never certain that the limitations are real until they are effectively probed) of those with whom they work. Young or middle-aged staff people may become intensely frustrated, even depressed, in recognizing the inability of their program to reverse the decremental aspects of aging for some participants. If their own desire to see greater forward movement is thwarted, they may give up the challenge of working with the elderly and turn to fields in which they feel that more can be accomplished. Researchers frequently share these feelings; so do many physicians and other health-care personnel. Thus, the difficulties of the elderly exacerbate the difficulties of the elderly in circular fashion.

A Few More Words about Research

Much of the research in psychological gerontology has described ways in which older people differ from younger people. Sometimes the investigator takes the next logical step and seeks to identify those factors that produce age-related differences or age-related changes. Many gerontologists believe, however, that more emphasis should be placed on studying differences that occur between groups and among individuals of the same post-65 age cohort.

Is it possible, for example, that black Americans age differently than white Americans? We know that their life expectancies differ: black men and women have shorter life expectancies up until about 70 and longer life expectancies thereafter. We also know that they are susceptible to different diseases, that they live under different conditions, that they have much different life histories. Is their biological aging process different? Do they display different behavior and different performance levels when they become old? If so, why? Is it a matter of genetics? Different life experience? Different cultural expectations? All of these in combination?

But even this degree of differentiation is insufficient, because it lumps all members of one ethnic group together. Research should proceed to learn about the variation within the large and diverse community (or the many communities and individuals) of black Americans. What kinds of parent-child relationships develop between middle-aged, middle-class blacks and their elderly parents? In what ways do these resemble and differ from the relationships found between low-income blacks and their elderly parents? Or among middle-income whites? Asian Americans? Latin Americans? Polish Americans? Why?

Ethnicity, of course, is not the only possible basis for looking more closely at group differences among the elderly. The major thesis here is the existence of a need to look at the variability in behavior of individuals within each group and of subgroupings within each group.

The Demography of Aging

In 1974, a shade over 10% of the more than 200 million people in the United States were 65 years of age or older. In 1900, only 4% of the population were in this age group. Projected percentages for 1980 and thereafter are over 10%; if the present low birthrate should decline still further, it will have the effect of boosting the proportion of older Americans still higher. Comparable percentages characterize other industrialized nations, some being slightly higher. In nonindustrialized nations, the proportions tend to be lower (see Table 1.1).

Population Statistics

Factors affecting the proportion of older people in a population are numerous, only one of them being the obvious matter of changes in life expectancy. In-migration and out-migration can also have a substantial influence; one of the major reasons that the percentage of older persons was so low in the United States at the turn of the twentieth century was the constant influx of large numbers of European immigrants, mostly people of working age. Conversely, today, the Farm Belt states of Iowa, Nebraska, South Dakota, and Missouri, along with Maine, have the highest proportion of elderly—not because living in those states is so healthful (although this factor might contribute) but because younger people have been moving out. One exception: in 1972, Florida had the highest proportion of older persons

Table 1.1. Percentage of the elderly in the populations of selected nations. From the *Demographic Yearbook,* 1971, Statistical Office of the United Nations, Department of Economic and Social Affairs (United Nations, 1972).

	Percentage of Entire Population over Age 65	*Percentage of Persons over Age 65*	
		Males	*Females*
Hong Kong (1970)	1.4	81	19
Colombia (1964)	2.9	46	54
Iran (1966)	3.4	59	41
Mexico (1970)	3.7	48	52
Kenya (1969)	3.9	57	43
Turkey (1965)	3.9	43	57
Japan (1970)	7.0	44	56
Canada (1971)	7.9	45	55
New Zealand (1969)	8.1	40	60
Malta (1970)	9.0	44	56
United States (1970)	9.9	42	58
Sweden (1970)	13.7	45	55
Austria (1970)	14.1	38	62

(15.5%), because of in-migration. California and Arizona, both favorite retirement states, have 65-plus proportions below the national average, and Hawaii's 6.1% is higher only than Alaska (2.5%); unlike Florida, these three vacation states attract very large numbers of younger in-migrants.

Another important determinant of age-cohort proportions is the birthrate. The nations with lower levels of industrialization tend to have a high birthrate; today, with improved maternal and infant care, a much higher proportion of those born live to maturity. As a result, the proportion of elderly in their populations has diminished (although the actual numbers have increased).

Individuals born in the United States in 1900 had a life expectancy at birth of 47.3 years, with women expected to outlive men by two years (from National Center for Health Statistics, U.S. Department of Health, Education, and Welfare, 1971). Their counterparts born in 1971 were estimated to have a life expectancy of 71, with women outliving men by 7.4 years. This amazing increase in anticipated longevity, however, is largely the result of reduced deaths at early ages; therefore, the life expectancy of those born in 1900 when they attained the age of 65 was 12 more years, whereas the anticipated life expectancy of people born in 1971 when they become 65 is only slightly higher, 15 more years. Whites were expected to outlive "all others" by 14.6 years in 1900 and by an estimated 6.7 years in 1971. However, the future life expectancy for blacks surpasses that of whites at about age 70, and the 85-year-old black man or woman will probably live longer than the average white of the same age by a year or more. Perhaps a selective factor permits only the healthiest and most resilient blacks to live to such advanced years.

Interestingly enough, considering the faith so many people have in medical research, life expectancy in the United States has remained almost constant since 1955, with a slight drop-off for older men (USDHEW, 1971).

A listing of additional population characteristics is necessary. Of every 100 persons over age 65,

> 43 are men and 57 are women;
> of the women, 21 are married, 31 are widowed, and 5 are single or divorced;
> of the men, 31 are married, 8 are widowered, and 4 are single or divorced;
> 31 of the men and 25 of the women live in their own homes, 4 men and 10 women live with relatives, 6 men and 19 women live alone or with a nonrelative, and 2 men and 3 women are in institutions;
> about half have had 9 years of schooling or less (half of those between 25 and 54 have had nearly 12½ years of schooling);
> 44% of the men and 17% of the women are active in the labor market between the ages of 65 and 69; these percentages drop to 18% and 6%, respectively, at age 70; in 1900, about 65% of the men and 8% of the women over age 65 were either working or actively seeking work (from information provided through the Administration on Aging, USDHEW, and by Herman Brotman).

One related issue just beginning to receive attention is the political ramifications of a much larger percentage of people over 65. Shortly before the 1971 White House Conference on Aging, some older persons began wearing lapel pins with the slogan "Senior Power." Although these were more laughed at by passersby than they were cause for concern, they presaged the potential political power of those in their later years, should they ever become a cohesive political force. Not only did the Gray Panthers subsequently emerge as a relatively militant political group, but the older organizations, such as the American Association of Retired Persons and the National Council on the Aging, became more aggressive in demanding rights and opportunities for the elderly. The future is likely to see an increase in such demands, made by older people themselves and forwarded by legislators who become aware of the voting power of the elderly.

Finances

Older persons, for a variety of reasons, have limited financial resources. The most obvious reason is the reduction in direct income as the result of their retirement, since Social Security payments and other pensions rarely approach their previous pay level. Also, most of today's elderly lack the formal education that has permitted their children and grandchildren to move rapidly up job and income ladders; neither did their best working years fall during the period when affluence was readily available. As new age cohorts move into retirement years, these factors are changing.

Even today, however, the overall financial picture for older persons, although improved over that of ten or 30 years ago, is hardly reason for enthusiasm. In 1972, when the median income for families with heads between 14 and 64 was close to $12,000, those with heads over 65 were receiving almost $6,000, just over half the amount earned by their younger cohorts. When this age bracket/income comparison is made among those who are not living with families, the proportion of the income of those 65 and over to the income of those younger drops to 48%, while the actual median income amounts to less than $2,400. Although the number of dollars has increased due to increases in Social Security payments, purchasing power has not gone up because of inflation-produced price increases.

The percentage of older persons officially judged "poor" dropped by about one-third (from 30% to 19%) between 1959 and 1972. However, the poverty was not evenly distributed across population groupings: 41% of older blacks were judged poor in 1969, although this percentage was down considerably from the 71% of 1959.

When older people themselves are asked how they feel about their finances, their responses do not require much sophistication to interpret. Prior to the 1971 White House Conference on Aging, nearly 200,000 questionnaires of persons attending state or community meetings preparatory to the conference were analyzed. Over half of these people received and spent less than $200 a month (in 1971); over one-third had trouble paying their housing costs; over half stated that they did not always have enough money to "make ends meet" (Institute for Interdisciplinary Studies, 1971). A 1969 study in the Detroit area came up with similar results: 57% of retired people felt their present finances to be inadequate (the median amount considered adequate to meet all needs being a modest $400 per month) (Peterson, 1972). Percentages may vary from study to study, and today's inflation may make these figures appear even more dramatic than they are; but the feelings of the elderly are beyond dispute.

In determining the standard of living of older persons, income from all sources is only one basis. How have their expense patterns been altered during their later years? Since Medicare was instituted, one major financial cost has been reduced for the elderly—a cost that, unlike food or clothing costs, tended to weigh heavily upon one segment of the older population at any given time, while only slightly upon the rest. A factor counterbalancing reduced health costs, however, is that inflation has eaten deeply into the resources of many older persons; and health costs have by no means disappeared, since Medicare covers only a portion of the total medical bill. Between 1960 and 1970, dental fees rose by 50%, physicians' fees rose by about 65%, and hospital service charges nearly tripled (U.S. Bureau of Labor Statistics, 1971; Consumer Price Index for 1970, cited in Chen, 1971). The cost of health services has continued to rise at a rapid rate since these data were collected in 1970, when Medicare, Medicaid, and public assistance combined paid only 65% of the health bills for those 65 and over (Chinn, Colby, & Robins, 1971).

Nonetheless, not all older people are poor. In 1972, of 7.6 million families with a head of household 65 or over, 18.5% had incomes in excess of $10,000, and 3.5% of these had incomes in excess of $25,000.

Younger people having limited financial means can always hope for future improvement; older people have no such hope for themselves. Ask the elderly what their greatest need is, and the answer is likely to be the need for additional money or the need for goods and services that can be purchased with money. The low income associated with old age comes at the same time that other resources diminish. A younger person can walk to save bus fare, but the older person may have difficulty in walking; the younger person can borrow money against future prospects, but the elderly have few future prospects of added income; the younger person can get a part-time job, but work is often not available to the older person.

Not only does the lack of money represent a limited potential for purchasing goods and services; in addition, some people in our society look upon poverty as either the fault of the individual or, in fewer instances, the will of fate or of God. Therefore, according to some those who are poor deserve to be poor, and many of the elderly themselves were brought up to accept this view. Poverty in old age thus is destructive of self-adequacy and self-esteem in many ways.

Health Statistics

Of the 1.7 million annual deaths of persons over age 45, 70% are caused by heart disease, stroke, or cancer, with heart disease accounting for 40% of all such deaths. Accidents and suicide, major causes of death in younger persons, continue to take a heavy toll in the later years, but their relative importance diminishes.

Both the incidence (the number of persons affected for the first time) and the prevalence (the total number of persons affected) of heart disease approximately double between the 45 to 64 age group and the 65 to 79 category; hypertension also increases by approximately 50%. Women suffer from both conditions more than men, and blacks are much more frequently afflicted than whites.

Some additional data:

Slightly over half of the 65-year-old population are edentulous (have lost all their teeth).

About three-fourths of all older women and over half of all older men have visual defects defined as moderate to severe (20/40 vision or poorer).

About 7% of older men and 5% of older women have severe hearing impairments (defined as 46+ decibels); over one-fourth of the remainder have mild or moderate impairment.

Over 25% of older men and nearly 10% of older women are unable to carry on major activities (such as work or housework) because of chronic health conditions; an additional 21% of the men and 30% of the women have some limitations, but not in major activities; nonwhites are more likely to be handicapped than whites.

Only 2% of persons in the United States over 65 are bedfast; 6% are housebound and another 6% are ambulatory only with difficulty (Shanas, Townsend, Wedderburn, Friis, Milhoj, & Stehouwer, 1968b).

The most common bases for limited activities are, in order of importance, heart conditions, arthritis and rheumatism, orthopedic impairments, and mental and nervous conditions.

Each year, about 15% of 45- to 64-year-olds are hospitalized; about 25% of those 65 and over are hospitalized; the average length of stay for older persons is a few days longer than that of younger persons; and nonwhites tend to remain hospitalized longer than whites (USDHEW, 1971).

How many older people are institutionalized? An estimated 5% of persons over 65 (1970 estimates) are in mental hospitals, homes for the aged and dependent, other institutions, and other "group quarters." Of these, half (2.4%) reside in long-term care facilities variously described as nursing homes, convalescent facilities, and so forth. The percentage increases sharply with increasing age.

There is a much higher rate of such institutionalization for women and a much lower rate for nonwhites. The former can probably be accounted for by the greater life expectancy of women and their tendency to be younger than their husbands. Women can care for their ill and dying husbands but, when their own health becomes seriously impaired, they are less likely to have a spouse available to care for them.

The matter of racial comparisons is more complicated. Some people believe that nonwhites "care for their own." It is a common assumption, perhaps with some basis in truth, that blacks and other minority-group members offer greater acceptance to their elderly and that both the older minority members and their families prefer that they remain within the home. This assumption has been attacked in recent years as an excuse on the part of the "white establishment" for not providing adequate long-term care facilities for nonwhites. The claim is made that nonwhites are underrepresented in these care facilities because of overt racial discrimination and because of serious economic limitations. The black elderly are found in these institutions at less than one-third the rate their population would indicate (Testimony to U.S. Senate Special Committee on Aging, 1971). The resolution to this conflict is still in the future.

Before leaving the topic of geriatric institutions, I wish to draw attention to another recent finding. Kastenbaum and Candy (1973) show that the 2.4% figure for all institutionalized elderly residing in long-term care facilities far underestimates the number of persons who—at one time or another in their later years—spend time in such institutions. By referring to death certificates and other data from the greater Detroit area, they found that approximately 24% of all deaths of persons 65 and over occurred in nursing homes and other long-term care facilities. These figures obviously underestimate the proportion of older persons who entered these institutions, since many died after having been returned to their own homes or to other forms of residence. Long-term care facilities apparently serve as a residence for at least one-fourth of all older persons at some time during their later years.

The effects of ill health, like the effects of low income, have many ramifications. One of these is that the elderly tend to suffer from chronic disease rather than from acute illnesses. Also, recuperation periods are longer; sometimes the course of the medical problem will not change for the better, and the older person simply has to find some way of adjusting to it.

There is no need, however, for the older person to become completely passive in response to changing health. He retains the ability to make decisions for himself, often right up to the point of death. One decision he may make is to remain physically active, to use the strength and energy that he has. Even in convalescent-care facilities, geriatric exercises help keep muscles flexible. An unaware observer might find the sight of an elderly person slowly raising and lowering his arms peculiar or even amusing, but the task is often a difficult one for the elderly person himself. And the more the body is capable of doing, the more effective the individual is in retaining mastery over his environment.

Some Final Comments

The previous pages are filled with numbers, dollar signs, life-expectancy rates, and other statistics that may be passed by as devoid of human meaning. They should not be. Each time a statistic is given, vast numbers of human beings are represented. If one-fourth of all people over 65 spend some time in a long-term care facility, the chances are 50-50 that one of your parents will be in such an institution (assuming your parents live to that age). If women outlive men by over seven years and if you, as a woman, find a male partner three years older than yourself, you can expect ten years of life beyond his death. If 18% of all elderly and 41% of elderly blacks are living beneath the poverty level, this means that the central part of the city you live in or near has large pockets where substantial numbers of older people live without adequate food or shelter, without access to transportation, with the most limited of recreational opportunities. Behavioral scientists, perhaps psychologists in particular, often prefer to deal with people at the individual level or in small groups. Yet if all the advanced-psychology undergraduate majors in the United States gave their entire annual income and one eight-hour day a week to individual interactions with the elderly, it would make only a modest dent in the social problem that exists. It is not my purpose to be either alarmist or defeatist. I merely wish to underline the necessity of having some grasp of the demography of old age in order to gain a frame of reference for understanding the behavior of individual older persons.

In the final analysis, then, you and I and everyone else are faced with two alternatives: to live old or to die young. When phrased in such abrupt terms, neither alternative seems appealing; yet those who have had contact with a wide variety of old people—both in institutions and out, both in good health and in less than adequate health—come away impressed by their ability to live with their difficulties and to enjoy life as much as, and often more than, younger persons, In the film *Gigi,* Maurice Chevalier sings a ballad, "I'm Glad I'm Not Young Anymore." The lyrics remind us that people in their later years are no longer susceptible to the anxieties and vanities and social pressures of their youth and middle age, that they *can be* more free to be themselves, to do what is important to them. As income, health care, facilities (such as transportation and housing), and general opportunities and options become more available for the elderly—and there seems to be a discernible trend in this direction right now—the later years can be a time of personal growth and satisfaction.

Chapter Two

Basic Processes and the Aging Individual

Why do people (and, indeed, all other organisms) age? Is aging really a natural process? An inevitable process? What can be done about aging to slow its pace or to eliminate it altogether (assuming that you wish to)?

First, we need to recognize two kinds of aging: *primary* and *secondary*. Primary aging is based on hereditary factors; secondary aging refers to the results of disease and to other causative factors that are not genetically based (Busse, 1969). Assuming that this two-factor approach is valid, we would need to drastically change both people's social and medical environment and their genetic makeup in order to eliminate aging altogether, although we might be able to affect the general course of aging by intervening either environmentally or genetically.

Factors in Aging

Although "nearly every environmental factor can influence the health, physical condition, and length of life of organisms, . . . certain of them are more important than others" (USDHEW, 1970, p. 21). The following are among those considered most significant.

1. Genetic inheritance. Exactly how genes affect aging is not known. Perhaps they determine the susceptibility of the individual to certain diseases; perhaps they influence the resistance of the person to what seems to be a "wearing out" of various organs; perhaps other effects are responsible.

2. Physical environment. Physical environment includes environmental temperature, mechanical forces (bumps, bruises), radiation, and

toxic substances (air pollutants, tobacco, pesticides, and various forms of bacteria and microbes). It could be extended to include housing, neighborhoods, and related aspects of the physical environment that affect longevity directly, by influencing health, and indirectly, by mediating the satisfaction of psychological and social needs.

3. Nutrition. People who lack an adequate diet most certainly die sooner than those whose diet is sufficient. Too much food, especially too much animal fat, also appears to be related to high mortality rate, although the evidence is not yet conclusive.

4. Medical care. There seems to be little doubt that both good preventive health care and good treatment affect longevity.

5. Physical exercise and activity. These factors seem to promote health and, therefore, longevity, although some care should be taken that the exercise is not unduly demanding for the individual's age and physical condition.

6. Stress avoidance. Psychological and social stress may speed up the deteriorations of aging, whereas emotional health and stability may slow them down. The issue of stress is a most controversial one in the health professions, and the mechanism through which stress operates in the aging process is not fully understood. Perhaps stress affects the circulatory system and, therefore, the heart and the free flow of oxygen to the brain; perhaps it affects the digestive system, so that the body's efficiency is reduced; perhaps it induces some as yet unknown, biochemical change, that, in turn, reduces the body's resistance to disease or reduces its recuperative powers when disease or accidents occur.

Therefore, if you wish to intervene in your own aging process or in that of others, you can contemplate doing so by altering the diet, the physical environment, the kinds of physical activities, the level of psychological stress, or by altering the genetic makeup, or whatever it is within the organism that is affected by the genetic makeup. However, although we have a reasonably good idea of what constitutes physical health and a minimally adequate idea of how to achieve emotional health, we know relatively little about how to translate this knowledge into longer life.

Our present concern, however, lies more with the psychological causes and ramifications of aging than with those that are strictly biological. This is an admittedly artificial differentiation, since a psychological alteration must always be accompanied by some biological change (if only hidden in the convolutions of the brain or represented in a momentary alteration in the nervous system); at the same time, biological changes often lead to observable changes in overt behavior, feelings, and attitudes. (For those who wish to read about biological changes in aging, see *Developmental Physiology and Aging,* by Paola S. Timiras, Macmillan, 1972, or *Time, Cells, and Aging,* by Bernard L. Strehler, Academic Press, 1962.)

The interaction between the biological and biomedical aspects of aging and its psychological and social aspects is great. On the one hand, the impact of physical illness or appearance change on behavior and attitudes is well known and obvious, in spite of substantial individual differences. On the other hand, a person's ability to find involvement and meaning in life probably has a major influence on some of the biological and health-related changes often associated with age. The statement "aging is a state of mind," although appealing, is a misrepresentation of what occurs; to say that "aging is affected by one's state of mind" is probably accurate. For some people, the commonly noted signs of aging may be significantly altered by a warm human relationship, by ability to find new meaning in life, or by involvement in some activity.

With our present limited knowledge, we often don't know whether a particular change is inevitable in the aging process, or whether available forms of social, psychological, or medical intervention might slow down the process, stop it altogether, or even reverse it. For example, it is unlikely that my gray hair can be returned to black (except through cosmetics), but I could slow down my loss of lung capacity by exercising more, and a good program of recreation and activities might reverse my increasing tendency to disengage from social interactions. (There is speculation that even gray hair can sometimes be altered by improved diet, suggesting that environmental factors come into play here also.) A friend of mine, who also tends toward disengaging, could probably be helped to a richer life if he could only be persuaded to use a hearing aid; he takes good care of his hair, so his baldness is probably beyond further control; but his loss of teeth could be slowed down, perhaps stopped altogether, if he would undergo periodontal surgery and follow a moderately demanding dental-maintenance program.

Describing the kinds of deficits that occur with aging, especially those that become most evident during the sixties, is only the first step in ascertaining their meaning to the individuals themselves. We must ask a series of questions that are generally applicable to all forms of age-related change.

1. Does it matter? Granted that we can accurately measure innumerable age-related changes, do these changes necessarily have a meaningful impact on the lives of the persons affected? Substantial hearing loss obviously does; so does severely reduced short-term memory. But how important is reduced olfactory capability? Or sensitivity to temperature change?

2. Does it imply other changes of a more serious nature? A relatively rapid decline in certain types of cognitive capacities may be indicative of cardiovascular or other health problems, perhaps prognostic of more

serious illness or even death. Another change may signify little of importance for the future.

3. Will an intervention alter the path of the decrement? Will a surgical procedure, or any health treatment, serve to ameliorate the problem? Will improved social relationships, the re-establishment of feelings of personal meaningfulness, an increase in sensory or cognitive stimulation, or any other planned intervention make any difference?

4. Is there any mechanical device that can help? Can the problem be helped or corrected by eyeglasses? A hearing aid? An artificial limb?

5. How is the individual coping with his losses, and how can he be enabled to cope more effectively? Three people suffering the same hearing loss will respond in three different ways. Person A obtains a hearing aid and begins to learn lipreading; he remains reasonably cheerful. Person B refuses a hearing aid and retreats into a solitary life; he becomes depressed. Person C also rejects a hearing aid, but she manages to find a friendship group that will accept her hearing loss and make the important adjustments themselves.

Although the changes to be described in this chapter are frequently biologically based and are often beyond our present ability to alter effectively, each organism that is affected is an individual with a unique life history, a unique personality constellation, and a unique set of present circumstances. Each alteration, then, has a unique impact on the individual affected.

Often the greatest problems arising out of reduced capacities and lowered performance-effectiveness are their effects on the person's self-concept and social interactions with others. These losses can readily inhibit a person's behavior in such a fashion that his overall adjustment is affected. Reduced visual acuity, if extreme and not fully correctable, can make reading difficult or impossible, can reduce a person's mobility by making driving impossible, and can deny him the pleasure of watching movies or television. Moreover, each change is a reminder of the aging process that is causing it, and these decrements can be frightening as predictors of things to come.

Fortunately, people are reasonably resilient, and most older persons come to peace with such changes by recognizing that the only way to enjoy life is to cope with the changes as effectively as possible, compensate as much as is appropriate, and then go on to other matters. Also, except for those whose losses are premature or extensive, each aging person notes that others in his age cohort are encountering the same difficulties. In a very real sense, this knowledge is supportive; it can lead to a preference for social contacts within his age group rather than within more vigorous, often less understanding, younger and middle-aged groups.

Sensory and Psychomotor Processes

A large variety of sensory processes have been noted to show decrement with age, with the decrement tending to accelerate when individuals reach their sixties and thereafter. Since virtually all the research on sensory processes has been cross-sectional, we need to be somewhat cautious in interpreting the findings, but there is little reason to believe that longitudinal research would substantially alter the obtained evidence concerning patterns of change.

Visual Capacity

The eyes perform a variety of tasks in interaction with the perceptual processes occurring in the brain; these interactions produce visual images that you now perceive. You must be able to see near objects and far objects, monochromatic scenes and color scenes, objects in an almost completely dark room and objects caught in the sudden blaze of strong light. What are you able to see in the later years?

One of the most obvious changes is the reduced capacity to see objects near at hand, due primarily to the loss of elasticity of the lens (MacFarland, 1968). Thus, older people tend to become farsighted; this fact gives rise to their common complaint, often but not always made facetiously, that telephone books and road maps "must be using smaller print these days." Eyeglasses can normally correct this deficit.

The ability of the eye to adjust to changing amounts of light also diminishes with age. Both adapting to the dark and adapting to the light are involved; the older person is less likely to make either adjustment as efficiently as before (MacFarland, 1968). Whereas eyeglasses can help problems of distance adjustment, devices to compensate for the loss in ability to adjust to light are not available, and the practical difficulties that arise can be considerable, not only for certain professions (such as aviation) but also for night driving. At night, the driver must be able to adapt rapidly to the headlights of an oncoming vehicle without being blinded by the glare and then, with equal rapidity, readapt to being able to see the dark road and surroundings. Decreased ability to make these adjustments is one of the reasons that older persons often avoid driving at night.

Difficulty in adapting to glare increases rapidly beginning in the forties; peripheral vision begins to show meaningful decrement in the fifties and sixties (MacFarland, 1968). Again, the implication for older drivers is obvious: increased difficulty in perceiving the danger signals of a car approaching from an angle or coming up rapidly in an adjacent lane.

Overall visual acuity also becomes less accurate with age; such losses increase exponentially beginning in the fifties. By age 65, about half of all persons have a visual acuity of 20/70 or less, some five times the proportion of those who have that degree of visual loss at age 45 (National Center for Health Statistics data, cited in Riley et al., 1968). The ability to perceive depth with accuracy also diminishes with age (Bell, Wolf, & Bernholz, 1972), and some loss of color-perception acuity has also been found (Corso, 1971).

Reading about all the kinds of age-related decrements can be intimidating unless you return to the questions we asked earlier and deal with each decrement separately, while recognizing that substantial individual differences in reactions do exist. Although all the decrements I described can have a meaningful effect if they are severe enough, many can be corrected or compensated for, while others may have only a negligible impact. Wearing eyeglasses can usually correct inadequate visual acuity; learning techniques of driving at night will help compensate for some of the adaptation problems; being careful to move your head to compensate for reduced peripheral vision can reduce the burden of this change.

Not only the older person but the rest of us, as well, who help shape his environment, need to be aware of ways to compensate for these age-related changes. For example, improved design of vehicles and housing will eliminate some sources of difficulty.

So far the discussion has centered on visual decrements that, for the elderly population as a whole, often have no major impact on behavior and functioning. What about severe visual impairment? An interview study conducted by the National Center for Health Statistics in 1963 and 1964 found that the proportion of older persons unable to read newsprint was over ten times that of all other individuals. Of the 500,000 legally blind persons in the United States, approximately half are over age 65, and over half of the newly reported cases of blindness come from this large age group (White House Conference on Aging, 1972). Incidence of extensive loss of visual acuity is twice as high among the nonwhite population as among whites, with the ratio for absolute blindness greater than three to one (USDHEW, 1966).

All in all, blindness and other serious visual impairments affect more than 7% of those between 65 and 74 and 16% of those 75 and over (based on 1957–1958 data reported by National Center for Health Statistics, cited in Riley et al., 1968). The need for these people to develop effective coping behavior to deal with their deficits is considerably greater than for individuals undergoing the normal changes of aging.

Audition

Patterns for hearing resemble those for vision. Although decreases in auditory sensitivity are relatively slight during the early and middle adult years, loss of acuity is more extensive for tones in the higher ranges (Corso,

1971). Thereafter, as with visual acuity, decrements accelerate at later ages.

An obvious result of hearing deficits is increased difficulty in understanding speech. Older people frequently ask others to repeat what they say or to speak louder or more distinctly. Research has shown that when speech was clear, undistorted, and presented without competing noise, older subjects suffered very little loss in ability to understand. "As the difficulty of the distorted and noise-masked speech became greater, however, very large differences were revealed between the auditory performance of the young subjects and those in their later years" (Bergman, 1971, p. 150). Often the hearing loss distorts only certain frequencies, so that shouting does no good —it merely amplifies the confusion.

Hearing impairments in those over 65 are much more common than visual impairments, reaching 13% of those between 65 and 74 and 26% of those 75 and over (National Center for Health Statistics, cited in Riley et al., 1968). Of an estimated 4.5 million persons with a serious hearing loss, some 55% are over age 65. These findings parallel those concerning the prevalence of visual disorders.

Although the visual deficits of the elderly are generally believed to occur through disease and general deteriorative processes, and, to a lesser extent, from accidents, hearing loss is probably more closely linked with environmental variables, such as the much-discussed "noise pollution." An investigation of hearing among the Mabaan tribesmen in North Africa showed much less hearing loss with age, including reduced loss in the higher frequencies, than among residents of major urban areas (MacFarland, 1968). Mabaan tribesmen obviously differ in a variety of ways from residents of the comparison cities used in the study (New York, Dusseldorf, and Cairo), so it is difficult to pinpoint the specific bases for their good hearing; but this study at least helps to point up the crucial nature of environmental factors.

Hearing loss, perhaps even more than visual loss, isolates individuals from their social groups. The problems of communicating to someone hard of hearing may be immense, and people suffering hearing deficits late in life are much less likely than younger people to learn lipreading or signing.

Other Sensory Modalities

Other sensory modalities have not been extensively studied, and findings are inconsistent and piecemeal.

Taste. We have only contradictory information on taste. Some studies show decrements and others show no changes. Studies of the taste receptors themselves show progressive degeneration, which, in combination with decreased salivary flow and other factors, may account for older people's frequent complaints that their food is tasteless or requires heavier seasoning (Corso, 1971). Taste sensitivity itself shows no significant decrement until the sixties (Corso, 1971). Unfortunately at this time of life, other health problems may require elimination of salt or strong seasonings from the diet—another example of the double bind in which the elderly find themselves. The tongue does not show meaningful anatomical degeneration until the seventies or thereafter (Birren, 1964). One study did find that sensitivity to all four taste qualities (sweet, sour, bitter, salty) did diminish after the late fifties (Cooper, Bilash, & Zubek, 1959), but since later research (Glanville, Fisher, & Kaplan, 1965) indicated that moderate and heavy smoking decreased taste sensitivity over time, the evidence for a basic, rather than an environmental, degenerative process is still not established.

Smell. Again, the evidence is contradictory. Although anatomical changes in the olfactory receptors suggest probable loss of sensitivity, research is meager (Birren, 1964).

Pain. Once more, contradictory information. A brief review of relevant literature (Riley et al., 1968) cites one study showing increased sensitivity, four studies showing no differences, and two studies showing decreased sensitivity. The difficulties in conducting research on taste, smell, and pain are great: for example, do you accept the report of the individual on when "it hurts"? If not, what criteria can be established? Adaptation to pain, tastes, and odors also makes such research methodologically difficult.

Touch. Very little research has been done, but there is some suggestion of decrement in tactual sensitivity (Corso, 1971).

Vestibular senses. Dizziness is more commonly found among older people than among other age groups and is one of the major causes of injury and death from falls. As people become older, they are more likely to become dizzy while looking down a staircase and then trip or fall down the stairs. Another common source of falls is misjudging the last step. Deaths from falls among those 65 and over occur more than twice as often as traffic deaths, and the ratio jumps to four to one at age 75 (Rodstein, 1964).

Older people have been found to sway back and forth more than younger people, both when their eyes are open and when they are closed. This finding supports the assumption that some deterioration of vestibular function accompanies aging (cited in Szafran & Birren, 1969). Accidental injuries and deaths from falls could be reduced by proper illumination, effective use of colors for top and bottom steps, use of nonskid floor waxes, and care in laying and tacking down rugs and carpeting (Rodstein, 1964).

Dizziness or vertigo worries older people more than is often recognized. In their study of geriatric health in the United States, Denmark, and England, Shanas and her associates (1968b) noted that dizzy spells are much more closely associated by the elderly with self-ratings of poor health than is blindness. This comparison held for all three nations.

Psychomotor Performance

Decrements with age in psychomotor performance resemble the decrements in sensory capacities. Older persons, on the average, have less muscular strength, take longer to react to many forms of stimuli, take longer to make a motion, and are generally less capable of performing athletic tasks such as running, swimming, or boxing (Birren, 1964; Riley et al., 1968).

The major issues, I feel, are not whether these changes occur—they most certainly do—but why they occur, whether their decremental course can be altered, what implications the changes have for life satisfaction, and what coping mechanisms can be most usefully employed. As these issues are discussed, it will become increasingly evident that psychomotor performance cannot be considered in a vacuum but must be inter-related with sensory functioning, cognitive abilities, motivation, personality, and the social setting.

Birren (1964) emphasizes the need to differentiate between speed and timing: the former refers to "the fastest time in which a task can be performed" and the latter to "the sequential relationships between parts of a task" (p. 112). Timing appears to be the more complex phenomenon.

The major basis for the increased slowness of performance with age is generally assumed to be changes in the nervous system. ". . . The evidence indicates that all behavior mediated by the central nervous system tends to be slow in the aging organism" (Birren, 1964, p. 111). This slowness comes about as a result of "loss of cells and age changes in the physiological properties of nerve cells and fibers" (p. 111).

Although average changes in speed and timing can be charted across an age span, the changes vary greatly as a function of the individual and of the nature of the conditions under which the task takes place. Even younger persons who show signs of certain medical conditions such as cardiovascular problems or arthritis take longer to respond than age peers who are unaffected (Spieth, 1964). One experiment compared older individuals with a group of younger ones from which athletes had been excluded; response-time differences between age groups were greatly reduced, indicating that exercise may be a significant factor (Botwinick & Thompson, 1968).

Other contributing factors may include personality characteristics leading to caution or enthusiasm (clinical observations often suggest, for instance, that older people lack the enthusiasm of younger people; this factor, if true, may affect speed of performance). Older people may also lack motivation to achieve in the laboratory setting, in which most such studies are conducted.

Factors relating to the task conditions have also been investigated. If the task is familiar, well practiced, and not complex, age-related differences are minimized. The same holds true for tasks for which subjects have the proper set and for which the stimulus is strong and unambiguous (Birren, 1964).

Practical Application: The Older Driver

The research findings discussed in the previous pages have great applicability both to understanding of the older person and to immediate and highly practical situations. Although implications for work, for leisure and play, and for gardening and home maintenance (which are work for some and play for others) are obvious, I will use the older driver as an integrating example, largely because the tasks involved in driving are both more familiar and less complex than the tasks involved in work.

According to our previous discussion, older drivers should have a higher rate of accidents than younger drivers. After all, they have greater trouble accommodating visually to varied distances, take longer to adapt to dark and light, suffer from reduced visual acuity and poorer hearing, are more susceptible to dizziness, experience slower reaction times, and—not previously mentioned—evidence greater susceptibility to confusion in the face of multiple concurrent stimuli—for example, having to deal simultaneously with rapid traffic flow, freeway on- and off-ramp signs, honking from other cars, and directions given by a passenger. On the other hand, they generally have had many more years of driving experience and tend to be more cautious than younger people in their driving habits.

As part of a test program (Case, Hulbert, & Beers, 1970), seven drivers over 51, with an average age of 65, and three younger drivers (50 and under) drove a specially equipped vehicle in which a variety of measures of their functioning and performance could be obtained. Although the sample in this study is extremely small, some of the results are interesting enough to consider. For example, the mean speed for the younger drivers was slightly—but significant statistically—faster than for the older drivers; the older drivers depressed the brake pedal more often; the older drivers had a significantly slower heart rate than the younger drivers (not an anticipated result); and the older drivers changed their rate of speed more often. These and related findings, by and large, suggest greater caution on the part of older drivers. The conclusions of these investigators were that older drivers monitor themselves effectively and accommodate well to their sensory and motor losses, while their judgment remains as good as that of younger drivers. Only when events occur too quickly for them to adjust do older drivers do less well than younger ones.

What about accident rates? It all depends on what you use as the measure. That is, if your accident rate is based on accidents per 1000 persons within an age group, accident rates for the elderly are low; if the rate is based on accidents per 1000 drivers within an age group, accident rates are moderate; if the rate is based on accidents per miles driven, older drivers have a very high accident rate. With fair consistency, accident rates per mile for ages 70 to 79 equal those of teenagers; but drivers 80 and older have still higher accident rates (Planek, Condon, & Fowler, 1968; Riley et al., 1968). Older drivers are more likely than chance would indicate to end up in accidents through (1) failing to yield, (2) turning improperly, and (3) running red lights; their accident rate from speeding is relatively low, however. When asked what bothers them most in driving, older drivers list lane-changing, making left turns, and parking. All of these tasks involve turning, which the data indicate is the second most frequent cause of accidents among the elderly (Planek et al., 1968).

Unlike auto accident rates, industrial accident rates show little or no change with age, although the types of accidents do change. Accidents caused by poor judgment appear to decrease with age, whereas accidents caused by sudden events, such as falling or being hit by objects, increase with age (Riley et al., 1968). These data are basically consistent with those for vehicular accident rates and with what we know about the functioning of older people.

Given the information we have on older drivers, what kinds of decisions need to be made? Should older drivers be tested more frequently? Should they be given limited licenses permitting them to drive only at certain hours or in certain kinds of traffic? Should their insurance rates be altered? Should they be kept from driving at all? Should individual terms of freedom to drive be arranged for them, based on each person's accident rate and driving-test scores? (Keep in mind that we seldom do that for younger drivers.)

The significance of being able to drive an automobile is considerable. For the older person who can afford to maintain a car, driving permits him to shop, visit friends, take a drive in the country, or get to an appointment. In short, it provides great freedom. Not being able to drive severely limits the options open to older people. They must walk, find adequate public transportation (often not available), take taxis (often too expensive), or depend on family and friends. The loss of a driver's license is also symbolically important: it represents the loss of immediate freedom and the potential loss of future freedoms. It deprives the individual of something that has probably long been taken for granted; it signifies the loss of one measure of independence, mastery of the environment, and social status.

Other Implications

The human significance of loss in sensory and motor capacities, like the significance of any loss, is often far greater than the immediate difficulties that arise from functional changes. A person who has spent many years playing tennis begins to find his game no longer improving or even remaining constant. He has more difficulty moving his arms and legs, fatigue occurs more quickly, his ability to follow the ball after an opponent's smashing serve is no longer as good, his game as a whole seems thrown off, and he may begin to play much more conservatively. Although he may not notice these changes for some time, they are almost inevitable, and he is likely to lose much of his enthusiasm for the sport. Not only is he less likely to enjoy playing—a loss in and of itself—but he may lose his best opportunity for healthy exercise. When, in addition, he confronts the reality of his own aging process, the loss will be compounded. The friendships and enjoyable leisure, the beer following the game, and the shared camaraderie also cease.

If a person suffers from a decrement in hearing or from an arthritic condition severe enough to make walking or even buttoning his clothing difficult, the impact can be even greater. Even though decrements occur only very gradually and sometimes not at all, and even though substitute satisfactions are often readily available, we live in an era in which the notion of personal growth is extremely important. The realization that growth in certain tasks will no longer occur can be very depressing, especially since it often coincides with other losses, such as the death of friends or the recognition that another promotion will probably never be awarded. Coming to terms with these problems, while still being able to engage in substitute activities and retain a high sense of life satisfaction, is the major demand made on the aging. Trying to understand these processes and to learn how to intervene in order to slow down or reverse negative outcomes is a major demand made on the gerontologist.

Cognitive Capacities

When I was in my twenties and very early thirties, I had a distressingly accurate memory for both names and faces. If there were 20 people at a party, I would know the names of at least 15, and perhaps all 20, by the end of the evening, and I would remember at least half of them if I met those people at another party three months later. I could never comprehend why everyone didn't recall names as I did; I thought they just didn't care. Now, a couple of decades past the peak of my recall, I no longer seem to remember the names of people, and I must admit that my recollection for faces isn't any too good either. What has happened?

Has something happened in the initial learning process, so that the name, the face, and the association between them no longer get stored in my memory? Does something happen in storage, so that the images fade? Does something happen when I want to retrieve the information from storage, so that the name doesn't just fall out almost automatically, as it once did?

Or am I paying less attention? Is it simply less important to me to remember who's who? Have I become tired of knowing everyone? Was it all a game in the first place, and I no longer wish to play "Memory Names"? Or could it be that interference has been established—that I have learned so many names during my lifetime that the old recollections get in the way of new learning? Or, perhaps, that I have so many things on my mind, so many other tasks that draw my energies and effort, that name-remembering no longer has a sufficient claim on me?

Another idea is pervasive. If, indeed, my memory for immediate associations is not as good as it used to be, regardless of the reasons, has there been a similar decrement in my long-term or intermediate-term memory? Does this possibility have any implications for other kinds of cognitive processes? For problem-solving? For decision-making? For dealing with abstract issues? For grasping the significance of world events? For anything from my susceptibility to classical conditioning to my creativity to what I will term, for lack of a better word, my wisdom?

Moreover, why do some older people still have excellent memories (including both long-term and immediate memory)—much better than the memories of those 30 years their junior? Conversely, why are the memories of some younger persons so poor, even though their basic intellectual capacities seem adequate? To what extent do biological factors explain such occurrences? Psychological factors? Social factors?

Research in cognitive changes associated with old age—changes in conditionability, in rote memory, in serial and paired-associate learning, in decision-making, in creativity, in remembering and forgetting—is substantial. The results, although not necessarily contradictory, are very difficult to interpret. There is support for those who believe that capacities diminish, but support also exists for those who believe that capacities don't really diminish at all.

Methodological Considerations

Each area of study has its own methodological problems, but there are certain over-riding issues involved in the subject matter of cognition.

First, many age-related factors will cause a loss in certain kinds of capacities but not in other kinds. For example, someone suffering from Parkinson's disease will obviously not be able to accomplish certain motor tasks; even mild arthritis may cause a woman to do poorly in a timed task requiring movement; lack of sophistication in the ways of behavioral research may lead to anxiety, confusion, or resistance in older research participants, whereas young people today are undoubtedly much more research-sophisticated.

Second, cross-sectional research suffers from severe limitations when applied to the study of age differences in widely separated age cohorts. Several studies have clearly shown that cognitive changes over the years, measured longitudinally, suggest much less decline and, sometimes, no decline at all, whereas cross-sectional research using similar methodological procedures indicates substantial age-related differences. These studies are almost always carried out in laboratories or other formal settings, and the experience of younger people in formal learning settings is considerably greater than that of older people. This fact is as true today as it was 30 years ago (although it may not be so true 30 years from now).

Third, it is difficult to measure one cognitive process without inadvertently measuring others. If we are trying to measure immediate memory, our results may be confounded by the rapidity with which the information is presented; or, if we attempt to measure ability to learn a simple task, like learning nonsense syllables, we may end up with data reflecting reaction-time characteristics, perceptual and sensory limits, and anxiety. The results of one study suggest that older people fatigue more rapidly in experimental settings than younger people, and that learning differences may arise because most such studies take too long (Furry & Baltes, 1973). I would speculate that boredom and lack of motivation, rather than fatigue, might together constitute the intervening variable leading to age-related differences in findings.

Memory

An old war-horse in the stable of geriatric humor has one elderly person saying to another "I understand that three things happen when people age: their memory begins to slip . . . and I forget the other two." Like much humor, this quip expresses what some older people actually face.

"It is impossible to separate learning from memory in any but the most arbitrary way" (Botwinick, 1970a, p. 242). Any attempt to measure what an individual recalls depends on his ability to learn the material. One recent study concludes that "the decline with age in memory performance is attributable to the decline with age in learning performance . . . " (Moenster, 1972, p. 262). The investigator admits that not all studies support her findings, but she does cite several that do.

Although memory can be classified in numerous ways, it is commonly divided into immediate memory and long-term memory. Immediate memory usually involves recalling material for a brief period of time, after which it may be discarded or forgotten; long-term memory does not necessarily involve the intent to recall at a later time, but the material is nonetheless placed in one's cerebral storage area—to use the computer model—for later retrieval. By and large, laboratory studies of simple immediate memory show only slight evidence of decrement with aging, perhaps none at all. If there is any kind of interference with the simple act of memorizing, however, evidence of some age decrements does appear (Bromley, 1966). For example, the simple task of memorizing a series of numbers in sequence can be done by older respondents as readily as by younger ones. However, if the numbers are then to be recited backward, or if another task is imposed, such as sorting the numbers into classes, evidence of noticeable decline with age is found (Bromley, 1966). More complex tasks involving immediate memory produce more evidence of age-related decrements. Botwinick (1970a) states that the older respondents' performance decrement is caused by interference during the process of learning the materials and suggests that interference is more readily handled by younger persons than by the elderly.

The memorizing abilities of older persons are more affected when the materials to be learned are presented in rapid succession, when the materials are exposed briefly, and when the learning task is difficult (Botwinick, 1970a). These laboratory findings are consistent with the conclusions drawn by those who work with older people. Older people will often request that information be presented more slowly, and they frequently seem to prefer dealing with one piece of information at a time. Moreover, interruptions appear to be more disruptive for them than they are for younger persons. However, older people often develop devices for dealing with these changes, and—probably more importantly—most learning tasks in the real world do not require the kind of memorization used in the laboratory; that is, it is rare that someone needs to memorize a list of words or a series of numbers. When such memorizing is required, it is often in relation to a task, and the experience of the older person can compensate for his impaired memorizing ability.

Long-term memory presents even more serious methodological problems. An older person seems to recall events that occurred many years earlier with considerable clarity, but rarely can anyone around confirm the accuracy of such recollections. Also, because he has such long experience, an elderly person's remembrance of certain events and experiences can represent only a small number of recollections out of a vast reservoir of occurrences. Nonetheless, recall of early events is so commonly reported by older persons that we should probably take their claims largely at face value, withholding judgment on how large a proportion of these early experiences are forgotten and how much inaccuracy does enter the memory of these experiences.

Classical Conditioning and Instrumental Learning

Classical conditioning occurs when two stimuli, only one of which has previously led to a particular response, are presented close together in time. Through pairing with the first stimulus, the second comes to elicit a response identical to, or almost identical to, the response produced by the first stimulus. To move away from psychological jargon: a hypodermic needle thrust into the arm of an 8-year-old causes withdrawal, wincing, and sometimes tears. Eventually, the mere sight of the needle approaching the arm may produce similar withdrawal, wincing, and perhaps tears. The unconditioned stimulus is pain; the conditioned stimulus is the sight of the needle.

The conditionability of older people is considerably less than that of younger people (Schonfield, 1969); it takes more trials (experiences, associations) for the unconditioned stimulus to produce the expected response. These findings are important, because understanding the basis for these learning decrements may help us understand those organic changes in the elderly that unquestionably affect such learning.

Instrumental learning (also termed *operant learning*) is the basic paradigm for "behavior modification" and for some other forms of psychotherapy. In brief, instrumental learning occurs when four conditions are met: (1) the individual is motivated to do something; (2) he has the potential to produce the correct response; (3) when he gives the correct response, he receives feedback of results and some kind of reinforcement; and (4) if he does not give the correct response, he is motivated to continue to respond until he does. Many types of learning can be described as instrumental: learning to drive, learning to thread a needle, learning to please a teacher, or learning to swing a baseball bat (even though other kinds of learning may contribute in each of these instances).

Although there have been animal studies of age-related differences in instrumental learning, there has been virtually no research with elderly humans. Older rats learn less well under operant conditions than do younger rats, but we aren't certain about people (Botwinick, 1970b). Behavior modification principles have, however, been successfully utilized in altering the behavior of the elderly in a clinical setting (Cautela, 1969), but, in these experiments, no comparisons were made between the behavior of the elderly respondents and the behavior of younger people.

Complex Learning

Although verbal learning (learning to respond to the stimulus of words) in older individuals seems to be less effective than in younger individuals, much of the difference can probably be explained as a function of differences in memories and reaction times. Another possible explanation is the tendency of older people to be less willing to take risks, which suggests that their fear of failure may be greater than their need to achieve (Eisdorfer, 1969). For example, whereas younger persons, and especially college students, will take the chance of being wrong in laboratory studies, older persons are fearful that they will appear foolish when they make errors or inappropriate responses. As a result of inhibiting their rate of responding, however, they are less likely to accomplish the necessary learning (Eisdorfer, 1969). In reviewing the relevant literature, Botwinick (1970a) concludes that good health and a high measured intelligence (that is, IQ) reduce age-related differences in verbal learning, whereas greater task difficulty increases the differences. Most writers on this topic end their discussion by admitting that very little is understood about the phenomenon and that much more work needs to be done.

In discussing problem-solving, another author begins with the statement: "That there is a deterioration of problem-solving behavior with age has been amply demonstrated" (Canestrari, 1967, p. 65). He then offers several explanations for these changes: (1) interference, perhaps based on earlier learning, (2) rigidity, (3) reduced ability to abstract, (4) greater difficulty in organizing complex materials, (5) loss of short-term memory capacity, (6) defects in ability to discriminate between stimuli, (7) ". . . inability to delay responses because of defects of inhibitory processes" (p. 64), and (8) difficulty in disregarding irrelevant elements in the learning situation. Some of these reasons reflect deterioration in the central nervous system, but it is also possible that uncertainty regarding decision-making or difficulty in accepting failure—both of which are personality characteristics—may also be involved.

Intellectual Competence

As we move from the simpler forms of cognitive behavior, such as response to classical conditioning, to the more complex forms, such as intellectual functioning, the evaluation of age-related differences changes from difficult and uncertain to difficult and very uncertain. Not that there is any problem in ascertaining that decrements occur; they most certainly do. Rather, the cogent problem is answering such questions as why they occur, what causes them to occur for some persons and not for others, and why they seem to affect certain tasks more drastically than other tasks.

What is intelligence? Is it ability to succeed in an academic setting? To earn a lot of money? To have insight into what motivates other people? To relate effectively to strangers and friends alike? To know what to do under stress? To hammer a nail in straight? To memorize a page of text? The list could go on indefinitely. Perhaps all these elements are part of general intelligence.

There are several ways to measure intelligence. We can, of course, administer a test of intelligence, but not all intelligence tests give equal emphasis to the same factors. Some are largely measures of verbal skill, whereas others depend more on measuring memory, spatial perception, or arithmetic abilities. It is important to have a reasonable idea of which components of intelligence are being measured; it is particularly important when you are looking into age-related changes in intelligence test scores.

However, there are other ways to determine intelligence. You might decide that a particular older woman whom you know is wise and that her long experience has given her an ability to achieve her goals, to come to terms with herself and the world, to maintain high life satisfaction, to impart to others her accumulated wisdom and understanding. Her memory may not be too good, especially for recent events; her hand may shake a little when she drives; she may require you to speak a bit more loudly and distinctly than you usually do. But you develop the patience to accommodate to the older woman's needs because you enjoy and can profit from what she offers.

As difficult as it is to measure immediate memory or verbal fluency with accuracy, it is immensely more difficult—perhaps impossible—to measure wisdom. Although people will disagree on the adequacy of the measures of intelligence that are commonly used, they would disagree much more on any measure of wisdom. And, after all, the measure of intelligence that we now use can actually help us in seeing and understanding some of the changes that occur with age, as long as we recognize their limitations.

Cross-sectional studies of intelligence usually show that considerable decrement in intelligence accompanies old age. Longitudinal studies, however, indicate much less loss of cognitive capacity. In one follow-up of older individuals three years after initial testing, virtually no changes in measured intelligence had occurred (Eisdorfer, 1963); another study spanned an eight-year period and found decrement in only a few areas (Jarvik, Kallman, & Falek, 1962). Twelve years later, when respondents were in their mid-eighties, significant losses were found, but these could be explained largely by terminal decline (see p. 41) (Blum, Fosshage, & Jarvik, 1972).

These studies reveal certain patterns of change. Verbal ability declines much less than psychomotor performance; tested abilities that require speed or that depend on immediate memory decline more than those that are untimed or that depend on experience. Tests of general information and vocabulary frequently show evidence of increased capacity with age, particularly if the differential levels of the respondents' formal education are controlled. However, speed does appear to be the major factor, to the point that Jarvik and Blum state that "decline on speeded psychomotor tasks represents a normal concomitant of aging, while decrements in cognitive functioning are pathognomonic of cerebral disease" (1971, p. 205). Also, men's speed declines more than women's, a finding that is interpreted by the investigators as representing the greater likelihood that men are experiencing terminal decline (Blum et al., 1972). The common belief that older people diminish in capability may reflect (1) people's observations of the very old, (2) the substantial numbers affected by terminal decline, (3) some modest decrements that many suffer, and (4) the prejudices and expectations of the perceiver.

The concept of crystallized versus fluid intelligence is helpful in integrating the various kinds of age-related intellectual changes. Fluid intelligence refers to those capacities that develop relatively independently of the cultural milieu, such as associative memory, intellectual speed, inductive reasoning, and memory span; crystallized intelligence includes those capacities that are strongly affected by the culture, such as verbal comprehension, general factual knowledge, and social awareness. Fluid intelligence "enables the person to perceive and discriminate between things, to discern relationships and groupings, and to work out implications creatively and productively" (Bromley, 1966, p. 248). Crystallized intelligence permits the individual to utilize his experiences and "to progress to more abstract and complex forms of learning and thinking ... " (p. 248). Changes in fluid intelligence are assumed to have a neural base and are often found in younger persons suffering brain damage. Therefore, among the aged, we often find reduced abilities for complex decision-making, speed, and some forms of perception. But little or no loss, or even slight gains, are observed in verbal comprehension, social awareness, and the application of experience. When we associate both forgetfulness and wisdom with the elderly, we are reflecting these two broad classes of intellectual capacities.

Creativity

Creativity has been the topic of considerable writing and research, but very few studies relate to older people. One widely cited investigation (Lehman, 1953) determined the age at which well-respected persons in different fields made their major creative contributions. Although its findings varied somewhat from field to field, they left little doubt that creative high points occur in the younger years. Lehman's work has one important methodological flaw, however, that requires comment: most good scientists and artists discover a new approach when they are fairly young and then begin to develop the various ramifications of that approach. If they neglect this subsequent development, the significance of their original work may never be noted, since it is often the accumulation of creative accomplishments, not just one such accomplishment, that signifies a real contribution. When the *total* creative output of each noted scholar, artist, and scientist is considered, it is the fifties and not the thirties or twenties that account for most of these people's richest work. Furthermore, considerable productivity continues well into the sixties, the seventies, and, occasionally, beyond (Dennis, 1966).

The Possibility of *Terminal Decline*

In the preceding pages, I have described many changes that are commonly associated with human aging. I believe that changes arise to some degree from genetic programming and to some degree from environmental influences. Individual differences are great as to how much each of these forces influences the human organism. For Person A, loss of hearing may be largely the result of inherited qualities; for Person B, the hearing loss was due to an accident to the eardrum; for Person C, the decrement came about from working where loud noise was constant. Similar illustrations could be provided for other kinds of change.

One correlate of age-related change is only recently being recognized; it is called *terminal decline.* This rather strange term refers to observations, well substantiated by research (for example, Riegel & Riegel, 1972; Jarvik & Blum, 1971), that individuals who show a notable change in any one of a variety of measures of cognitive performance are more likely to be dead within a few years than are those who show no particular change. This observation suggests that many (but not all) kinds of intellectual decrements may be the result of the same factors that will eventually lead to death; perhaps the significant losses of intellectual abilities are prognostic of death even before medical diagnoses can be made.

Assume, for example, a ten-year longitudinal study of changes in cognitive performance, beginning with people who are 60 years old. When the participants are tested at age 65, there will be a moderate decline in average scores. When they are retested at age 70, some of them will have died or will be very near death. If we eliminate these persons from the sample and then reanalyze the data from the first five years of the study, the decline shown in cognitive performance will be minimal for those remaining in the sample. The implications are clear that physical health, and even health-related matters that are not obvious, have a great impact on cognitive functioning. Perhaps changes in cognitive functioning do not result from aging *per se* but from changes in physical health that frequently occur among older people. More research along these lines is required before we can feel comfortable with these tentative conclusions.

Implications of Cognitive Changes

Eisdorfer (1969) summarizes his own thinking in a helpful fashion:

> However, nothing . . . should be construed to indicate that there are no truly age-related changes in intellectual and cognitive functioning. Loss of neuronal tissue, change in the metabolic rate of the brain, loss of circulatory capacity, all lead to a level of primary change. The fact remains . . . that we know little about many of these phenomena, and how much they would affect behavior in the absence of other complicating social and psychological variables [p. 247].

When people do find themselves less able to remember events, names of acquaintances, or books they have read, and when they do realize that their problem-solving behavior appears less effective than it was in earlier years, they respond in a variety of fashions. One response may be to withdraw from activities or people offering potential stress; another is to become irritable or angry, to insist that what they remember is correct; a third is to increase dependency on family members, friends, or professionals in order to compensate for their own deficits. It is little consolation for these people to learn, for example, that cognitive decrements occur not so much with age as with cerebrovascular problems, since the changes are equally real in either event. And older people are hardly comforted by learning about terminal decline, although this matter is of major importance to gerontologists, who can investigate ways to intervene in the course of whatever medical changes are accruing.

Society builds in certain protections against having to confront such losses in its older citizens. No matter how devastating retirement is for some people (see Chapter 5 for fuller discussion), it removes an aging person from competing with younger people whose cognitive capacities are not yet declining. Also, allowance is often made for some forgetfulness and uncertainty on the part of the older individual; since an older person's forgetfulness may be seen as typical of his age, it does not usually serve as a basis for teasing him or for assuming pathology in him, as would similar behavior in a younger person. However, younger people often stereotype the elderly and presuppose decrements that have not really occurred.

On the whole, of course, any kind of reduction in cognitive competence is likely to reduce the options open to the older person. To the extent that the elderly do become forgetful and are aware of this forgetfulness, they are deeply concerned, often anxious, and sometimes frightened. Some have the fear, not entirely without justification, that their confusion is a sign of more confusion to come; others worry that they are becoming senile or "crazy."

Whatever concern they feel regarding decrements in cognitive capacities, most elderly people recognize that they must cope with this difficulty, and many do so very effectively. Humor is one method of coping; older people themselves constantly joke about memory problems. Another method is the simple expedient of writing things down rather than trusting them to memory. A third approach is exerting extra concentration on matters that need to be recalled. Other strategies used depend on the individual and the situation.

Basic Needs

In the traditional introductory psychology course, heavy emphasis is placed on the basic *needs* (or *drives* or *motives*) that must be satisfied in order to maintain the biological stability of the individual organism. Of these, the most researched appears to be hunger, but a substantial literature is also available on thirst, sleep, and—to a lesser extent—temperature regulation, air hunger, and others. Sexual activity is often included as a need, although it relates to the maintenance of the species rather than to that of the individual. Sometimes, needs that may or may not prove to have a biological base are also discussed, such as the needs for activity, for exploration, and for satisfaction of curiosity.

In spite of the apparent importance of these matters to psychologists, these needs have certainly not caught the attention of psychological gerontologists, although they may be more significant than is generally realized.

Hunger

The professional literature says virtually nothing about age-related changes in the intensity of the hunger drive, although a great deal has been written about nutrition. Since older persons, by and large, use up fewer calories, it might be assumed that their caloric intake diminishes with the years, and that is probably what happens. If taste buds do, in fact, become less sensitive, this calorie reduction might not be as painful as it sounds. Of course, the social enjoyment of eating with others, the retention of familiar eating habits, and other personal factors often will compensate for lack of appetite.

Food has very important meaning to people, over and above its nutritional value. "Breaking bread" is an ancient symbol of welcome and trust; certain foods have prestige (for example, white rice may be strongly preferred by older Asian Americans, even though brown rice is more nutritious) or rich cultural associations (for example, the "soul food" of the black American or the traditional cooking of Jewish or Mexican or Italian families).

Eating is a highly social event, and numerous federal programs have attempted not only to provide nutritious meals for low-income elderly people but to encourage them to use these meals for pleasant social interaction. The eating habits of older people living alone are often erratic. It is not uncommon to find an elderly man or woman, residing in a small apartment, eating directly from a can while standing in front of the refrigerator. Often, no semblance of a balanced diet is observed. Meals are sometimes skipped or consumed at irregular intervals. (This is not necessarily a poor practice, but one wonders what such people do about the medicines that their physician has instructed them to take before every meal.)

Recent recommendations state that five smaller meals a day are usually preferable to three larger ones (Howell & Loeb, 1969), and that undereating is undoubtedly preferable to overeating or even, perhaps, to eating to the point of being moderately "full." In experiments with lower forms of life, life span was extended by reducing the normal dietary intake, particularly by reducing the amount of proteins (Barrows, 1971).

Sleep

Older people often take naps, frequently by falling into a light sleep in the middle of a television program, while reading, or even, occasionally, while talking. On the other hand, they frequently claim to sleep less at night, so perhaps the total amount of sleep doesn't change much. Insomnia is also common among older people, but I couldn't find any good study comparing the rates of insomnia for different age groups.

Sex

Sexual behavior among the elderly is frequently a source of humor. The jokes seem to fit largely into two categories: (1) he thinks he can, but he can't; (2) everyone else thinks he can't, but he does. Interestingly enough, I rarely hear a joke about sexual behavior in elderly women.

While there is no doubt that sexual activity drops off with age (Riley et al., 1968; see also Kinsey, Pomeroy, & Martin, 1948; Kinsey, Pomeroy, Martin, & Gebhard, 1953; and Masters & Johnson, 1966, 1970), there is considerable controversy over why this reduction occurs. The changes are undoubtedly biogenic to some extent, but psychological and social factors also contribute. Older people are undoubtedly responsive to the stereotype of themselves as incapable of sexual expression. Sometimes the physical attractiveness of available partners may be limited, and simple boredom with one's spouse is sometimes cited. Moreover, the early socialization process of today's elderly was often sexually constricting.

In spite of general decrement in sexual activity, active participation has been found in men and women in their seventies and eighties; those who are married have a decidely higher incidence of sexual activity than those not presently married. In a longitudinal study (Pfeiffer, 1969), between 20% and 25% of the men and a very small percentage of the women (ages ranging from 45 to 70) were found to have an increasing incidence of sexual interest and activity as they became older.

The Meaning of Aging to the Individual

The inter-relatedness of all human behavior is frequently emphasized by those studying psychological gerontology. We cannot discuss intelligence without questioning the role of memory, the meaning of changes in physical health, the impact of reluctance to take risks, or the importance of earlier schooling. And I could add other topics for study of intelligence in the elderly: mental illness, feelings of loneliness, simple lack of caring whether they do well on the tests, and failing vision and hearing. (Many persons with hearing loss either are not fully aware of their problem or choose to pretend they have full acuity; if they don't hear the instructions for tests of learning or intelligence, they "fake it.")

Again, let's return to a question I've asked before: assuming that we accept all the decrements described previously (even though the research is itself somewhat in conflict), what difference do they make in the day-to-day behavior of the older individual?

My opinion, which is shared by many and perhaps by most gerontologists, is that the behavior, performance, and life satisfaction of older people are less influenced by the measured decrements uncovered by our research than initial logic suggests. Anticipation is frequently more frightening than actuality, although declines and losses, when extensive, are objectively as well as subjectively important.

In spite of very real problems, the aging individual does appear to cope amazingly effectively with these losses. The following are some of the reasons.

1. These decrements often occur very gradually, and the aging individuals can adapt to slight changes almost without being aware that they are adapting.

2. Other people of their own age are also showing the same signs, and this fact is communicated among them, sometimes openly but often more subtly. An excellent example of open communication was given by Senator Ervin of North Carolina while chairing the Watergate investigation of 1973, when he learned that an attempt had been made to discredit him by digging up scandals or other evidence of misbehavior on his part. The 76-year-old senator quipped: "When I was asked about this, I said it didn't disturb me at all because . . . I deeply regretted to say that all the indiscretions I had committed were barred by the statute of limitations and the passage of time, and that I had lost my capacity to commit further indiscretions" (*San Francisco Chronicle,* June 30, 1973, p. 5).

3. Some evidence is available that older people (and, undoubtedly, younger people as well) can adjust to chronic problems and continue to enjoy life, even though the same problem might have appeared overwhelming when it was initially noticed. One study (Shanas, 1962) showed that people who had been afflicted with a chronic health problem rated their health as better than did individuals who were just beginning to confront such difficulties.

4. These decrements and losses are only one aspect of life. If other aspects are satisfying, the importance of the deficits probably lessens. For example, if family relationships remain rich, or effective substitute activities are available, the pain and reduced functioning of an arthritic condition will seem more bearable. (Again, please remain alert to individual differences.)

5. A form of rehearsal for later age roles often occurs. That is, older people are cognizant of forthcoming decrements, partly because they do notice minor changes when they accumulate sufficiently, and partly because they have observed the aging process in other individuals. Many of the elderly, then, have in a way rehearsed what it will be like to be older and thus have anticipated and planned for the discomfort of the actual changes.

In no sense am I suggesting that these physical and mental changes are unimportant. And their importance is made greater by the fact that they are often accompanied by the loss of familiar social roles, the death of close friends and family members, increased social isolation, reduced income, and other difficulties. My major thesis is that the elderly do have personal resources that enable them to continue to function with amazing effectiveness in spite of a variety of decrements and losses, and that those working with the elderly should make a greater effort to help them utilize residual personal strengths rather than bemoan such losses.

Chapter Three

Aging, Self, and Personality

What were you like ten years ago? What are you like today? What took place during those ten years that changed you from what you were to what you are? What accounts for these changes? To answer these questions is to gain some insights into the impact of aging on the self and the personality.

To grasp what happened during the past decade, you must examine more than one dimension of your past existence. It is immediately obvious that you have had ten years of experiences—pleasant and unpleasant, exciting and boring, warming and embittering, ego-building and ego-destroying. These experiences have helped to mold the person you were ten years ago into the person you are today.

But these experiences affected an already-formed organism, a human being who not only is acted upon but acts, a person who is not a helpless pawn of fate but someone with some degree of power and influence in shaping his own existence. Therefore, you must examine your last ten years of experiences, as they act upon you and are reacted to, in terms of your extant personality.

Moreover, the biological component of this organism that is you has also been changing. You don't look the way you did ten years ago: your weight, hair color, stamina, hand grip, sleep pattern, body contour, or physical health—any one or several of these—may have changed notably in ten years.

And society reacts to you differently. Your various positions and statuses have been in the process of change. You are no longer a student but an employed person; not unmarried but married and a parent; no longer financially dependent on older people but living on your own resources; no longer the child of two healthy parents but the emotional support of your widowed mother. Others expect different role-behavior from you as a result of your new positions in society, and you probably expect it from yourself.

Furthermore, the world has changed. The politics of the past ten years have included scandals and wars, peace treaties and political upsets, attempts to establish new political forms, and failures in some of these attempts. New forms of familial and community living have been tried; some have failed and others have endured, although frequently in altered form. The technology, advertising, ecology, and health care of today are not those of ten years ago. Not just the world at large but your own personal world, too, is considerably changed. You are probably not living in the same residence you were living in ten years ago; you have lost touch with some of your closest friends of a decade ago; people you know have married, and some have divorced; they have embarked on careers and changed careers, have had serious accidents or attempted suicide, have won contests and been on television. And all these changes of the past decade have interacted with each other and with your self-concept—with what you think and feel about yourself—to make you what you are today.

The same constellation of forces leads to age-related changes at any point in the life cycle, but the specific elements of these changes differ according to the time in life in which they occur. To understand the individual at 60 or 70 or 90, we also need to look at his experiences and personality, the relevant biogenic changes he is undergoing, changes in social positions and roles, situational changes arising in the world at large and in his personal world, and his changing self-concept. In this and the following chapters, the book's focus will shift to a discussion of the personality and the social environment of the elderly.

Adult Socialization

"*Socialization* is the . . . process whereby people learn the attitudes, values, beliefs, knowledge, and skills that allow them to become more or less able members of society. Socialization can mean learning an orientation, or a particular pattern of behavior, or a *manner* of acting" (Atchley, 1972, p. 159).

Laymen, as well as behavioral scientists, have come to recognize that the life experiences of individuals are greatly influenced by the groups within which they function, especially during their earlier years. Social class, ethnicity, nationality, rural or urban residence, and other associations of the early years are constantly noted in the literature. Yet, when comparisons are made among age groupings, differences in early associations are often ignored, while the spotlight is turned almost exclusively upon the meaning of being a particular age *today*.

Socializing Forces in Three Generations

A person born in this country in 1898 has had a different life experience, and certainly a very different upbringing, than has someone born in 1926 or in 1954.

The father was born in 1898; as a child he had no telephone, movies, airplanes, automobiles, running water, or—very likely—electricity. His country was not a world leader, had no race problem it was aware of, had no income tax or Social Security, and was not cognizant of having urban problems. Most likely Father was from the farm or a small town, raised Protestant, knew no Jews and few Catholics, and had never considered the possibility of a black man as a peer. After finishing ninth grade, he went to work, just in time to enter the armed forces for World War I. At 22, mustered out, he re-entered the work force, married, had children, bought insurance, and eventually voted for a chicken in every pot. At the age of 31, with two small children and vocational skills developed on the job, the stock market crash wiped out the investment money he has been speculating with, perhaps forced him to lose his insurance policies, and scared the hell out of him. At 35, the world caved in, and he was jobless, with a 15-year-old and a 10-year-old to take care of. Giving him the benefit of the doubt, let's assume he quickly landed another job, and that he managed to keep his family going, although it was pretty much hand-to-mouth for a while. In his early forties, he left his job for war industry and, for the first time, was covered by Social Security. However, in spite of a few good years, he was tossed back into the job market at the age of 47, without salable skills. He did get another job, or perhaps remained with his previous company at somewhat reduced status, hung onto the low-paying job, and managed to retire in 1963 with a modest amount of Social Security, a small house with the mortgage nearly paid up, a married daughter, and a son with two years completed at State University whose starting salary on his initial job nearly equaled his father's highest salary. Now he hears talk of urban renewal, ecological disasters, negative income tax, Black Power, sexual equality, communal living. The entire value system he felt comfortable with seems distressingly challenged.

The son has had a much different life. Still a child during the Depression, he has some vivid images and remembers that his family had very little money to spend. He recalls being urged to get an education so that he could obtain a good job and never be unemployed, and he was pushed to do well in school. He went into the armed service just in time to catch the GI Bill, and he spent two years in college before dropping out to take a job. His life has been a series of steps up the economic ladder, and it seems logical to him that study and hard work should do for everyone what it did for him. After all, his father was poor and uneducated, but made the necessary sacrifices to do a good job of raising two kids. So Son works, achieves, purchases, buys on credit, improves his housing and his automobiles, and decides that his children will go to the best college possible and will move up even higher. He has worked hard to earn what he now enjoys and, although fleeting images of Depression days occasionally disturb him, he feels as secure as his credit payments and health permit. Although not a churchgoer, he has internalized many of his father's traditional Protestant beliefs, and he expects his children to do so also.

The third generation you all know. But, as I described Generations I and II, I might have been describing the backgrounds of two social-class groups or two ethnic groups. Today we are so alert to social-class and ethnic differences in values that it seems strikingly naive to ignore the fact that age-cohort differences have the same impact [Kalish, 1969a].*

Socialization is commonly considered to occur in childhood, but in actuality it is a never-ending process. The grandfather described above was socialized in early childhood to look upon aging and the elderly in a particular fashion; but, as he himself aged, both his changing age status and the surrounding social milieu impinged upon his early socialization and altered it in various ways. When he reached the age of 77, his views of life and his behavior, although perhaps still bearing the impact of his early years, reflected a lifelong process.

People are constantly being socialized to new positions and, as a result, to new role-behavior. Leaving high school and entering the job market, the individual is now in a new social position, and accompanying this position is a new set of expectations for behavior, attitudes, values, performance, and so forth. Those who go to college, who marry, who enter military service, who end up in an institution of some sort, who drop out of society to drift or to work in a commune—all find that their new positions call forth responses and expectations different from those they have encountered, and their behavior very probably undergoes some changes.

Table 3.1 shows some of the age-related functions believed to be age-appropriate by one group of respondents. You may have different ideas, but you are still very likely to expect a person to "act his age." If he deviates from your expectations in a positive fashion—if you meet a physically vigorous 70-year-old who camps out and takes long hikes—you may be pleased that he is acting out of age sequence. More often, however, the deviation is perceived as negative. When a 50-year-old man is seen as behaving the way a 70-year-old is assumed to behave, people will comment disparagingly about "how fast he has aged." Or, if a 50-year-old woman continues to behave like a teen-ager, "Who the hell does she think she is?"

Age roles differ from culture to culture and from era to era, and most people are effectively socialized to the particular age role prescribed for their age group in their society. When they reach retirement, they become socialized to that stage. Their behavior in retirement reflects their earlier—even their childhood—expectations regarding appropriate behavior for retired persons, working in interaction with their accumulated life experiences, their personality, and their current contemporary expectations.

*From Kalish, R. A. The old and the new as generation gap allies. *The Gerontologist,* 1969, **9**(2), 83–89. Reprinted by permission.

Table 3.1. Consensus in a middle-class, middle-aged sample regarding various age-related characteristics. Fifty middle-aged men and 43 middle-aged women were asked to indicate the age for which each of these statements is most descriptive.

	Age Range Designated as Appropriate or Expected	Percent Who Concur	
		Men	Women
Best age for a man to marry	20–25	80	90
Best age for a woman to marry	19–24	85	90
When most people should become grandparents	45–50	84	79
Best age for most people to finish school and go to work	20–22	86	82
When most men should be settled on a career	24–26	74	64
When most men hold their "top" jobs	45–50	71	58
When most people should be ready to retire	60–65	83	86
A young man	18–22	84	83
A middle-aged man	40–50	86	75
An old man	65–75	75	57
A young woman	18–24	89	88
A middle-aged woman	40–50	87	77
An old woman	60–75	83	87
When a man has the most responsibilities	35–50	79	75
When a man accomplishes most	40–50	82	71
The prime of life for a man	35–50	86	80
When a woman has the most responsibilities	25–40	93	91
When a woman accomplishes most	30–45	94	92
A good-looking woman	20–35	92	82

From Neugarten, B. L., Moore, J. W., & Lowe, J. C. Age norms, age constraints, and age socialization. *American Journal of Sociology,* 1965, 70, 710–717. © 1965 by the University of Chicago Press. Reprinted by permission.

A quarter of a century ago, the elderly in one typical rural community studied were socialized to be active in church, spend much time with age peers, develop a special interest, such as gardening or a hobby involving collecting things, be deeply concerned about grandchildren (or great-grandchildren), retain contact with grown children but maintain considerable autonomy, and avoid financial dependence as long as possible (Havighurst & Albrecht, 1953). The situation today may not be very different, but now the values described above must compete with more contemporary pressures: to be politically aggressive, to receive religious sustenance through televised sermons in order to avoid dealing with urban transportation problems, or to turn to television-watching as a hobby rather than participate in more active involvements.

Age-related role-constraints are not inflexible, and the aging individual has considerable latitude in performing his proper role ("proper" is, of course, defined by a variety of forces in the community). Therefore, the particular pattern that a person follows in becoming socialized to the 65-plus role is a highly individual matter. Indeed, many observers feel that being elderly is a roleless role—that the position "old" is essentially defined by all the tasks and involvements and meanings that "old" is *not* and by very few that it is. Often, those tasks that have personal meaning (such as work, church involvement, family responsibility, sexual activity, anticipation of future growth) either are not available to the older person or are available only in much-reduced form. I feel that this view is unduly pessimistic, but it most definitely operates for some individuals.

Aging and the Sense of Community

Ask someone to tell you who he is in a series of phrases. He or she will probably respond by citing sex, education or vocation, ethnicity, national origin, religion, community, and, eventually, age. The designation "old" or "elderly" is often not highly salient for people who would normally be thus defined. Anyone who has worked in a senior center or other program or facility for the elderly has heard the comment "I don't want to be around all those old people"—even though the speaker is himself chronologically older than most of those he is referring to. Many people in their sixties and seventies refer to themselves as middle-aged.

Being socialized to the age role of "senior citizen" is often perceived as a step down in status and power. The behavior, values, and performance levels expected of this role can easily have negative valence, and this age group is the only one from which there is no escape. People often dread this stage in the life cycle; younger people frequently comment that they would rather die young than live to be old (and some elderly people concur).

The elderly do not possess the attributes of a minority group. They don't share a distinctive and separate culture. On the one hand, membership in their group is almost universal; on the other hand, it encompasses only one part of the life cycle (Streib, 1965). But the most important reason that this age group is not perceived as a minority group is that "the aged have little feeling of identification with their own group; they have a low degree of collective consciousness; hostility toward a depriving out-group is exceptional. The aged are not organized to advance their own interests and are not particularly attracted to such organizations" (Streib, 1965, p. 46). These statements were made about a decade ago. They may be less true today. Even so, I have—at least to date—seen little of the sense of "we-ness" among the elderly that is necessary to turn an aggregate of individuals into a group.

Personality Characteristics

Although each individual, regardless of age, is unique and can be fully understood only in terms of this uniqueness, we often describe people in terms of salient personality characteristics or qualities, even while recognizing the inevitable oversimplification that results. Some of the adjectives applied to the elderly are cautious, rigid, wise, patient, irritable, and forgetful.

Do these adjectives accurately describe personality changes that accompany old age? Although behavioral scientists have traditionally emphasized change processes that occur during infancy and childhood and have often ignored, or even denied, the possibility of meaningful change during the adult years, observers and theorists alike have recently come to view personality development as a lifelong process. The question that arises is whether the changes that occur when people enter their sixties are in any way predictable. In other words, is there any discernible change in personality that is likely to take place in older people in general or in any identifiable group of older people—such as women, grandfathers, Filipinos, Jews, introverts, college graduates, rural dwellers . . . ?

And, if such predictions can be made with at least minimal accuracy, what underlies the age-related changes? Are the changes inevitable, or almost inevitable, for all older persons who reach a particular age or who have a particular health condition or economic status? Are the changes most likely to occur only to the elderly in the Western world, or in the United States, or in the American middle class? Are the changes readily altered by planned interventions that are presently within our power to carry out if we allocate the personal and financial resources?

Furthermore, we may wish to differentiate between changes in personality that derive from the social and psychological aspects of aging and those that result from changing health or from retirement. For example, the fact that the elderly are more lonely than the nonelderly may reflect the greater likelihood that older persons will be living alone. Similarly, the fact that older people think more about their bodies is probably a direct outcome of their being more likely to have a chronic disease or to be uncomfortable or in pain. To determine which causal factors are attributable to aging *per se,* and which arise from events that accompany aging, is not always possible; but we could attempt to compare young and old retirees, or young and old with chronic diseases. Although methodological difficulties are considerable, such studies would at least shed more light on this confusing issue.

Research Findings and Age-Related Personality Differences

Although gerontologists consistently advocate the use of longitudinal research, very little has been done, and virtually no studies have been conducted over the period of time needed to determine meaningful trends. One exception was a major effort made to follow a group of elderly people in rural Pennsylvania over a 19-year period (Britton & Britton, 1972). At its inception, this project included almost all of the elderly living in the designated area. However, attrition through illness, death, and moving away left a very small number of people for the final analysis. Nonetheless, the results have meaning for our purposes. The most significant finding of the investigators was that, whereas some participants seemed to gain in personal strength over the years and others seemed to lose strength, otherwise "the positive-change people could seldom be distinguished from the negative-change people" (p. 153). Neither did the investigators' measures indicate any difference in this regard between those who died during the period of the study and those who remained alive. Given the competence of the initial planning and the effectiveness of the way the study was conducted, this lack of distinguishable group patterns demonstrates the complexity of predicting personality in late adulthood and old age over an extended time span.

Turning to the more numerous cross-sectional studies of age-related personality differences does not improve the picture to any great extent. Although a number of such studies have been conducted, relatively few personality characteristics have been evaluated, and the results on these seem to generate conflicting conclusions.

For example, one review of the literature concludes that sociability diminishes with old age, but the authors caution that the research they have summarized lacks methodological sophistication (Chown & Heron, 1965). Another overview of personality-research literature concludes that introversion does increase in the later years (Riley, Foner, & Associates, 1968), but a subsequent study showed no differences between young and old college graduates in their need for affiliation (Schaie & Strother, 1968). Virtually all of these studies are based on self-ratings by the subjects, but, since self-ratings are affected by inevitable biases, they require cautious interpretation.

If sociability does diminish with increasing age, does this fact mean that older people have less *need* for human relationships, or that they have less *opportunity* to participate in them? The results of research hardly clarify this issue. My own observations suggest that the psychological need for others does not diminish and may actually increase, but that older persons have lost many relationships through the deaths of others and through illness, both theirs and others'; they are less willing to make demands on friends for social contacts and less able, for reasons of money, health, and transportation, to follow up the potential relationships they do find.

In only a few instances are research results fairly consistent. Compared with people in general, the elderly do appear somewhat more cautious and less impulsive (Botwinick, 1970a; Chown & Heron, 1965; Riley et al., 1968); they are probably also more rigid and less flexible (Riley et al., 1968; Schaie & Strother, 1968); and they are more often depressed (Botwinick, 1970a), although their depression is often masked by attempts at denial and by the tendency of many people to ignore the complaints of the elderly (Goldfarb, 1967).

Over a decade ago, a particularly interesting study (Reichard, Livson, & Petersen, 1962) was conducted using 87 men over the age of 55, half of whom were retired and half still working. Contrary to the pessimistic expectations of so many observers and research investigators, the findings, based on many hours of interviews and tests with each man, indicated that those who were both older and retired (1) had greater ego strength, (2) showed less projection of hostility, (3) had fewer obsessional defenses, (4) were more open and trusting, (5) were less likely to reject women, (6) were freer from overt anxiety, and (7) had less hidden depression. The authors concluded that the period of greatest difficulty was the 64 to 69 age range, when the transition to new roles and circumstances was still in process. Once the transition had taken place, the strengths cited above appeared.

If you have found the frequently uncertain, conflicting, or ambiguous statements in this chapter irritating and frustrating, professional gerontologists and geriatricians certainly share your unhappiness. When we are discussing personality characteristics, personal-growth potential, adjustment, or self-concept, our need to avoid sweeping generalizations becomes extremely obvious.

Perhaps the multitude of factors that impinge on human behavior in the later years are not sufficiently taken into account. This behavior may reflect the immediate and specific situation, or it may reflect more enduring factors; but, in either event, few behavior trends show reasonable consistency, and their explanations often arise from other factors *related* to aging rather than from anything *intrinsic* to aging. They also appear applicable only in limited circumstances, not universally.

Adjustment and Growth in the Later Years

Adjustment refers essentially to one's effectiveness in getting along, dealing with the world, avoiding incapacitating social or emotional difficulties, and satisfying most of one's needs. "Personal growth" is a term that may encompass adjustment but goes further. It implies that individuals continue to make the most of their capacities, to develop their talents, and to act naturally and be themselves. Whereas "adjustment" can imply a static condition of no change, "growth" implies that change is ongoing and that this change is for the better, at least as the individuals themselves define "better."

A number of studies have been conducted on adjustment in the later years, almost all of them using self-ratings. A study of 118 people in Florida between 45 and 84 (Beckman, Williams, & Fisher, 1958) indicated that self-rated adjustment was lower among the older individuals but was higher among the better educated (although age and education were unrelated to each other in this sample). The positive relationship of adjustment to education was considerably higher than that of adjustment to age. Perhaps those individuals who pursued more formal education had more resources to begin with and, also, were provided more resources as a result of their education. Thus, participation in the educational process was both cause and effect of those factors that, in the later years, permitted better self-rated adjustment.

Personal growth makes more demands on the individual than does adjustment. Erikson (1963) believes that the major task for the later years is dealing with ego integrity versus despair. The older person must maintain the wholeness, the adequacy, the meaning of self in the face of stresses and losses that can readily bring about despair. Mixed with the innumerable tales of the personal deterioration of older people are many exciting accounts of people far advanced in age who continue to use their talents, to feel at home with themselves and the world, and to be and become the kind of person they want to be. Even when faced with death—sometimes even encouraged by the pressures of impending death—many people retain ego integrity. At the same time, the price of this integrity may be to reduce their attempts at active mastery of the environment and to gear themselves instead to passive adaptation.

The Changing Self-Concept

The self-concept is the image the individual has of himself; it reflects his actual experiences and the way he interprets these experiences, his actual self and the way he interprets this self. Two of the most important components of the self-concept are self-esteem and body image. Each of these is influenced by the aging process, and each, in turn, affects the psychosocial aspects of the aging process.

Self-Esteem

Given the stresses and losses that come with increasing age, given the lack of respect shown the elderly, given their diminishing physical capacities and sometimes their diminishing cognitive capacities, it is only common sense to believe that people's self-esteem should drop, perhaps drastically, as they enter their later years. Except that this common-sense conclusion is not borne out by the research data. When common sense and research data clash, we have three options: (1) to accept common sense, (2) to accept the data, or (3) to reconcile the conflict.

Some studies show evidence that self-esteem increases with age (Gurin, Veroff, & Feld, 1960), some show reduced self-esteem (Kogan & Wallach, 1961), and some show no change. In trying to make better sense of these data, a pair of Texas researchers (Kaplan & Pokorny, 1970) looked at the interaction among chronological age and other variables as they jointly affect self-esteem. They found several factors that helped explain previous inconsistent results (although their study hardly exhausted all the potential explanatory factors). First, for people who had not had any recent disruptive life experiences, age was positively related to self-esteem; for people who had encountered such experiences (such as business loss, death in family, loss of job), no age-related increase in self-esteem was found. Second, for people who felt they were living at about the same standard of living that they had anticipated earlier, self-esteem was higher among those 60 and older; for people whose standard of living was lower than they had anticipated, self-esteem for the 60-plus age group was lower; and even among those whose standard of living was better than they had anticipated, the self-esteem of older respondents was slightly lower. Third, having had a childhood fear of being left alone also proved significant; among respondents not recalling such a fear, the older group had higher self-esteem, and just the reverse was true for those admitting to considerable childhood fears.

Each of these findings makes sense. If the older people have a reasonably stable recent history, an anticipated standard of living, and no strong fears of being left alone, their self-esteem rises with age. Conversely, when disruptive forces occur, when standard of living is well below the level of aspiration, and when fears of being isolated and alone are strong, the older person is more vulnerable. This study suggests the need for future work in probing additional characteristics.

Another approach to the same problem was taken by Riley and her associates (1968) in their extensive review of the gerontological literature.

They juxtaposed a number of findings from various studies on self-esteem as a function of age. Compared to younger people, older individuals were (1) less likely to admit to shortcomings, (2) less likely to consider themselves in good health, (3) less concerned about their weight, (4) (among those still working) equally likely to view their job performance as adequate, (5) almost as likely to view their intelligence as being as good as others', (6) more likely to consider themselves as having positive moral values, and (7) somewhat more likely to feel adequate in their marriage or as parents.

Body Image

A healthy, alert man in his late sixties was asked by his son why he never went for a swim in the apartment-house pool, even though he enjoyed swimming and was quite good at it. The father explained that he was embarrassed to be seen in a bathing suit. When he was younger, he prided himself on being trim and lean. He was still slim, but his muscle tone had diminished, and the extremely common slight curving of his spine prevented him from standing as straight as he wanted to.

Physical appearance is important to most people, and, except for the occasional person whose face is judged "interesting," the physical appearance of an older person is not usually seen as attractive and certainly not as sexually attractive. Older people often make comments such as "When I look into the mirror, I see the face of an old person. It isn't me —I have the spirit of a young person." Or, "I am a prisoner of my body. It's not really me with arthritis, with sagging breasts and loose skin—it's someone else."

Again, the research findings do not confirm the hypothesis that older people are more concerned about their appearance than younger people. One study showed just the opposite (Maddox, 1963), and a recent investigation concluded that "a person's bodily worries and discomforts are not related to age *per se,* but reflect special life circumstances" (Plutchik, Weiner, & Conte, 1971). People with psychiatric problems are especially likely to be concerned about their bodies and appearance, and studies done in convalescent-care facilities are likely to include elderly people suffering from varying degrees of psychological pathology.

Explanations and Implications

Although helpful for understanding the changing self-concept of older people, the existing research is far from completely satisfying. To return to my earlier statement that "people's self-esteem should drop, perhaps drastically, as they enter their later years": why does research have to complicate and obscure the obvious?

One explanation lies in the research methodologies themselves. Perhaps the investigators are asking the wrong questions; perhaps elderly research participants are atypical older people, biased in the direction of having unusually high life satisfaction and morale; or, perhaps, older respondents distort their answers, either because they feel defensive or because they lack accurate insight.

Another possibility is that older people are comparing themselves with their own age group rather than with the entire age spectrum. They may not be considering their life situation in relation to what it once was or to what they would like to be but, instead, in relation to some of the difficulties they see their age mates encountering.

Another probable factor is the misinterpretation others often give to what the elderly say. Many people—professionals, adult children of the elderly, concerned observers—begin with the premise that self-esteem in the elderly is low. When these views are confirmed by the research or by the claims of the elderly themselves, the confirmation is accepted at face value. However, when older people deny that their self-esteem is low or that their self-concept is poor, these observers assume that the denial must arise from psychological defensiveness or from some form of conscious or unconscious distortion of their true feelings. Therefore, what the elderly say about themselves often makes little difference, since interpretation precedes observation.

An alternative approach to this issue is to assume that the elderly are indeed denying their own feelings of lower self-esteem, but that such denial is an appropriate and effective mechanism for adaptation at this point in their lives. Defense mechanisms perform an important function in permitting people, at any age, to maintain an adequate self-concept. Defense mechanisms can also promote difficulties. But we really have no sound information on their adaptive function for this age cohort and this context.

Another form of bias deserves more attention than it receives. Many people work with the elderly in settings in which they regularly encounter troubled older people. (Those who are physically well, socially and emotionally stable, and financially secure do not normally come to the attention of agencies and institutions.) Therefore, the professional social or medical or recreational geriatrician, who is a major molder of public opinion, interacts largely with those elderly people whose situations suggest that their self-esteem is below average for their age group.

All these factors undoubtedly carry some weight in explaining the discrepancy between research findings and common sense, but I feel that the comments in the previous paragraph on what could be dubbed the squeaky-wheel factor ("the squeaky wheel gets the grease") are insufficiently recognized by both professionals and nonprofessionals who work with the elderly.

Successful Aging

Success is in the eye of the beholder, and individual differences are as great in the perception of successful aging as in the perception of being a successful parent or salesman or politician. Four possible definitions of successful aging have been suggested.

1. *A way of life that is socially desirable for this age group.* This definition assumes that society in general knows what is best for older people. For example, if the weight of social pressure directs older people to be submissive, uncomplaining, accommodating, cheerful, and active in social organizations, these characteristics become the criteria for successful aging. The views of the elderly themselves, although reflected in this definition, are not paramount.

2. *Maintenance of middle-age activities.* This definition assumes that the more an older person functions and behaves as he did when he was younger—the more he is like a middle-aged person—the more successfully he is aging. This line of thought is age-ism at its worst, but it is implicitly (although rarely explicitly) accepted by many professionals and nonprofessionals. (Intriguingly enough, we often respond to young people on the same basis: that is, the more they resemble middle-aged adults in their behavior, demeanor, and values, the "better" they are.)

3. *A feeling of satisfaction with one's present status and activities.* This definition presupposes that older people's feelings of success primarily reflect how active they are and whether their health status, financial status, and so forth are adequate.

4. *A feeling of happiness and satisfaction with one's life.* This definition "assumes that a person who is aging successfully feels satisfaction with his present and his past life . . . " (Havighurst, 1961, p. 10). To measure life satisfaction, five components were defined and five relevant rating scales developed by one group of investigators (Neugarten, Havighurst, & Tobin, 1961). The components selected were (1) zest versus apathy (enthusiasm and ego-involvement versus listlessness and boredom, whether alone or in interaction with others), (2) resolution and fortitude (willingness to accept personal responsibility for one's own life versus either blaming oneself overmuch or placing blame on others), (3) relationships between desired goals and achieved goals (extent to which aspirations were accomplished during one's past lifetime and are being realized at present), (4) self-concept,

and (5) mood tone (happiness, optimism, and spontaneity versus sadness, loneliness, and bitterness) (Neugarten, Havighurst, & Tobin, 1961). These components should be of more than passing concern, because they have formed the basis for a great deal of research and speculation in social gerontology.

Any definition of successful aging actually turns out to be, at least in part, evidence of the values of the person offering the definition. For example, one highly active older woman decided that there was no excuse for any retired person's not making contributions of time and effort to the community, and she explicitly defined successful aging as the extent of this contribution.

Data gathered from lengthy interviews with 65 elderly people in San Francisco, half of whom lived in the community and half in long-term care facilities of some sort, showed that entertainment and diversions were the most frequently reported sources of high morale. Each of the factors shown in Table 3.2 reflects what these elderly respondents perceived to be successful aging for them (Clark & Anderson, 1967), but keep in mind that half of these people were in geriatric institutions.

Table 3.2. Sources of high and low morale for 65 elderly San Francisco residents.

Sources of High Morale	*Percentage Reporting This Factor*
Entertainments and diversions	69
Socializing	57
Productive activity	54
Physical comfort (other than health)	52
Financial security	46
Mobility and movement	40
Health, stamina, survival	20

Sources of Low Morale	*Percentage Reporting This Factor*
Dependency (financial or physical)	60
Physical discomfort or sensory loss	57
Loneliness, bereavement, loss of nurturance	50
Boredom, inactivity, immobility, confinement	38
Mental discomfort or loss	18
Loss of prestige or respect	12
Fear of dying	10

From Clark, M., & Anderson, B. C. *Culture and Aging,* 1967. Courtesy of Charles C. Thomas, Publisher, Springfield, Illinois.

The authors then developed six general themes, from the information shown in Table 3.2, that serve as the basis for high morale, life satisfaction, or self-perceived successful aging: (1) sufficient autonomy to permit continued integrity of the self; (2) agreeable relationships with other people, some of whom are willing to provide help when needed without losing respect for the aging; (3) a reasonable amount of personal comfort in body and mind and in one's physical environment; (4) stimulation of the mind and imagination in ways that do not overtax physical strength; (5) sufficient mobility to permit variety in one's surroundings; and (6) some form of intense involvement with life, partly in order to escape preoccupation with death (Clark & Anderson, 1967).

One particularly cogent issue regarding successful aging still remains unresolved and, indeed, virtually unexplored. People commonly assume that those who have led satisfying lives find it easier to grow old. They believe that these older people feel fulfilled, that they do not see themselves as cheated, and that they are able to reminisce satisfactorily. Moreover, they may well retain more resources—personal, spiritual, social, physical, financial—than do those whose young and middle years were less satisfying. Nonetheless, another kind of logic may be applied. For a highly energetic and active person, for someone who is productive and involved, the losses that aging sometimes brings can be even more destructive than for a person with more limited aspirations.

Earlier, I described an older man who was embarrassed to be seen in a bathing suit. Was his difficulty partly created by his remembrance of how good he once looked in a bathing suit? Is the person who never looked appealing better off when age begins to change his appearance? Similar questions may be posed when we consider the high achiever. The difference in accomplishments between work and retirement is slight for the low achiever, but the high achiever is removed from a major source of satisfaction when prevented from working. Are his earlier successes detrimental to his later feelings of success in aging? Or does the knowledge that he was once successful compensate for his current awareness that his potential for future achievement is limited?

This as yet unanswered question leads us to another concern: considering theme (4) above, can we provide any kind of planned intervention, educational or experiential, that will increase the likelihood of successful aging? These possibilities will be discussed in Chapter 5.

Disengagement

"I'd rather live a full life and die when I'm 40 than live until I'm 70 and watch the fullness of my life slowly dribble away." This and similar statements have been made by any number of 20- and 30-year-olds (although by very few 39-year-olds). Being fully involved and absorbed in life is often viewed as one criterion of successful *living* (see "zest versus apathy" above), but the picture grows hazy when we try to judge successful *aging.*

"At successive ages, people become more preoccupied with the inner life than with events in the external environment. . . . There is also less willingness to deal with wide ranges of stimuli or with complicated and challenging situations" (Neugarten, 1972, p. 10). At the same time that the individual is withdrawing from society, society tends to withdraw from the individual. This process of mutual withdrawal in the later years has been termed *disengagement;* it results in reduced social roles, social relationships, and feelings of meaningfulness in the elderly (Cumming & Henry, 1961).

Two kinds of disengagement have been described: (1) social disengagement, which refers to reducing the number and duration of social interactions, and (2) psychological disengagement, which refers to the person's reducing the extent of his emotional commitment or involvement with these relationships and with what is going on in the world in general (Havighurst, Neugarten, & Tobin, 1968). Although they are related, these two forms of disengagement are not identical. Some people have many social interactions but experience minimal personal involvement in them. Others have very few social contacts but may maintain a strong commitment to these few.

When the concept of disengagement was initially applied to the elderly, it was not only proposed as a descriptive theory of what occurs but also posited as an inevitable, natural occurrence (rather than one imposed by other individuals or by social institutions and forces), and it was thought to be a positive, adaptive approach to successful aging (Cumming & Henry, 1961).

There is "convincing evidence of decline in both social and psychological engagement with increasing age. Disengagement seems to us to be a useful term by which to describe these processes of change" (Havighurst et al., 1968, p. 171). Pressures on the older person and his social milieu to disengage from each other come from three related, but far from identical, quarters.

1. The social structure undergoes change. This process is evident when family roles, work roles, power sources, and so forth combine to place pressure on older people to restructure their lives. The older people's responses are likely to be in the direction of both social and psychological disengagement.

2. " . . . The aches and pains, the reduced energy level, the sporadic forgetfulness, the added nuisance of some chronic illness that must be coped with, all these turn the individual into himself and persuade those in his community to withdraw from him" (Kalish, 1972, p. 87).

3. With an increasing awareness that his future is limited and that death is not only inevitable but no longer far distant, the older person may be more likely to attend to himself and to whatever is extremely important to him, simultaneously pushing away whatever is not extremely important. The ultimate example of this behavior has been observed in the terminally ill patient who excludes from his bedside all but the two or three persons closest to him (Ross, 1969).

But to establish that disengagement occurs is not the same as to establish that disengagement is a natural or inevitable process, and most certainly not the same as to claim that disengagement is a positive aid in successful aging.

When disengagement does occur, it does *not* inevitably lead to successful aging. One study of 250 older people (Maddox, 1963) showed that their morale was directly related to their level of activity. Furthermore, increased activity levels over time were predictive of increased morale, and decreased activity levels of decreased morale. The majority of both popular and professional opinion supports the idea not only that involvement and activity are helpful in successful aging but that they may even help in maintaining survival itself. Nonetheless, one of the best studies on this matter (Havighurst et al., 1968) concludes that the data gathered by the authors support both the activity theory of optimal aging and the disengagement theory, ending with the statement that neither theory is sufficient to account for all changes that occur. The researchers postulate two concurrent forces within the lives of the older person, one pressing for withdrawal and enjoyment of a more leisurely way of life, the other requiring him to remain active in order to retain a sense of self-worth. And they also remind us that even those elderly who disengage from role-activities are not likely to disengage from the social values they have internalized over the decades. In the final analysis, disengagement is an inadequate response for some; for others, it is adaptive; and, for still others, it is merely the continuation of previously established behavior patterns.

Patterns of Successful Aging

As research on disengagement continues, it becomes increasingly obvious that neither the disengagement theory nor the activity theory is sufficient to define successful accommodation to aging. Following a different approach, Bühler (1961) describes four accommodation patterns, two successful and two much less successful. Older people may (1) wish to rest and relax, content that they have completed their necessary life work; (2) want to remain active and do so; (3) lack the strength, ability, or determination to continue their work (even though they are not fully satisfied with their accomplishments), but feel forced to accept their limitations and resign themselves, often unhappily, to their situations; or (4) feel frustrated and guilt-ridden, having led lives that they now find meaningless.

To these four patterns, I would like to add a fifth: (5) people may, regardless of the degree of previous satisfaction they experienced, find in their later years some meaningful activities or relationships that compensate for whatever changes old age has required of them. One such person, a retired economics professor who was in his nineties when I first met him, had spent over 20 years deeply engaged in raising chrysanthemums, developing hybrids, and establishing an organization for others who shared his love for these flowers. When a series of strokes forced him into a convalescent care facility, he continued to work in the institution's garden, regretting only that his 40 or 50 hours of involvement per week had to be diminished.

If you refer to the five criteria for life satisfaction listed above, you will note the relationship between the patterns Bühler considers most successful in aging (the first two) and Havighurst and his associates' notion that "zest" and "relationship between desired and achieved goals" are two major components of high morale.

Two other studies shed light on successful patterns of aging. Although both were restricted to relatively small numbers of participants, both sets of investigators spent a great deal of time with each subject. One project grouped people in five categories based on their adjustment to aging: (1) the mature type, (2) the rocking-chair type, (3) the armored type (those who depend on an elaborate set of defenses to ward off the anxieties of the aging process), (4) the angry type, and (5) the self-haters (Reichard et al., 1962). The terms are essentially self-explanatory.

In many instances, the person's mode of adapting to old age was a direct outgrowth of a long-term adjustment pattern. For example, the rocking-chair type "welcomed the chance provided by old age and retirement to take it easy. Society grants, in old age, permission to indulge needs for passivity and dependence that it does not grant young people. Thus they were free to be more truly themselves" (p. 130). This passage suggests that one kind of life-style is more adaptive for people's retirement than for their earlier years.

An inevitable hazard in such research is that the investigator, or other concerned persons who are primarily young or middle-aged (or, even, unusually active and engaged older persons), will define successful aging according to how *they* believe they will want to live when they are old. If not properly aware of this tendency, gerontologists and geriatricians may not perceive that many "rocking-chair" types have made a very adequate adjustment to aging. Many nonelderly people who are well aware of the difficulties the elderly experience in accepting the values and behavior of younger people are themselves unable to grasp what it would be like to be old. They fail to perceive that the elderly, even if they had been highly engaged in earlier years, might wish to withdraw or disengage to some extent. Similarly, highly active people of any age often have little sympathy and absolutely no empathy for people who prefer to avoid active involvement.

In the second project, Neugarten and her associates (1968) went a step further. They not only categorized personality types, but they related these types to role-activities and life satisfaction. Working with 59 men and women in their seventies, they found that those termed "integrated" all had high life satisfaction, regardless of the extent of their role-activity. The "armored-defended" elderly had high life-satisfaction levels if they were active, but two of the four people with low activity levels lacked high satisfaction. Among the "passive-dependent" and the "unintegrated," high activity levels were rare, and medium and low life satisfaction were common. These investigators concluded that "in normal men and women, there is no sharp discontinuity of personality with age, but instead an increasing consistency. Those characteristics that have been central to the personality seem to become even more clearly delineated, and those values the individual has been cherishing become even more salient" (p. 177).

Clearly, the relative roles that disengagement and activity play in the later years (and, very likely, throughout the life span) are only beginning to come into focus. The importance of these roles makes this area a fruitful and necessary one for continued investigation, through both formal research and careful clinical observation. Neugarten offers an appropriate concluding statement: "that there is no single pattern by which people grow old, and . . . older persons, like younger ones, will choose the combinations of activities that offer them the most ego-involvement and that are the most consonant with their long-established value patterns and self-concepts. Aging is not a leveler of individual differences except, perhaps, at the very end of life" (Neugarten, 1972, p. 13).

Mental Illness in the Later Years

Obviously, not all people age successfully. For some, the stresses and losses become too much, and—perhaps in keeping with earlier methods of coping with stress, or perhaps because the accumulated pressures are simply overwhelming—they display symptoms we would ascribe to *functional psychosis*. For others, organic changes in the brain lead to changes in behavior or mood, and these persons are referred to as suffering from *organic psychosis,* often resulting from *chronic brain syndrome* (which can also occur without psychosis). In 1968, approximately 128,000 people over the age of 65 were in mental hospitals, the majority being admitted for the first time after that age (Kramer, Taube, & Starr, 1968). Many other elderly people are undoubtedly mentally ill but are able to sustain themselves or be sustained by their families, or can be cared for in hospitals for acute or chronic illness or in long-term care facilities. Although a recent drop in first-time admission has been recorded for all patients, including the elderly, this does not mean that incidence of mental illness has decreased, but that admission policies of public institutions have changed. The highly disturbed elderly have been placed elsewhere, often in nursing homes, so that only the official statistics have changed, and not the actual problem. The rate of mental hospitalization is higher for older women than for older men; this higher rate may reflect the stresses of widowhood or, equally likely, arise from the fact that the elderly woman does not have a spouse available to care for her at home, whereas the elderly man often has a wife who is still living and capable of caring for him.

As more disturbed elderly persons return to nursing homes or to their own homes in the community, other community agencies have taken over the role once assigned to the mental hospital. There has been a "marked increase in the establishment and use of a variety of community-based facilities, such as outpatient clinics, day-care facilities, community mental health centers, halfway houses, and psychiatric services in general hospitals" (Kramer, Taube, & Redick, 1972, p. 441). Nonetheless, even though just 10% of the population of the United States is 65 or older and over 30% of the mental hospital patients are in that age bracket (Simon, 1971), the elderly account for only 2% of outpatient clinic patients, under 3% of day-care program patients in community mental health centers, and 4% of community mental health center care recipients (Kramer et al., 1972) —all of which certainly suggests under-utilization of these community facilities by the elderly.

Although the definition of "brain syndrome" or "chronic brain syndrome" is almost as controversial as the label "senile," the terms have not yet been replaced. And there is little doubt that this kind of condition accounts for the vast majority of new admissions to mental hospitals and, even, that it affects the majority of patients over 65 who reside in mental hospitals. This diagnosis, like many, can be misleading, because organic brain change and actual behavior do not always show a close relationship. Some people whom autopsy showed to have extensive brain damage had displayed no meaningful behavior change, whereas in others, who exhibited all the symptoms of extreme chronic brain syndrome, autopsy showed little actual brain change (Simon, 1971). Moreover, we frequently find that persons diagnosed as senile are able to improve greatly under the proper supportive program. Diagnosing people as senile may be a self-fulfilling prophecy, since these people are likely to be ignored by treatment programs and, instead, placed in physical and social environments that provide no stimulation and thus exacerbate their symptoms.

Symptoms of chronic brain syndrome include impaired memory, altered cognitive functioning, depression and emotional instability, delusions and hallucinations, and significant behavioral changes, caused by either senile brain disease or cerebral arteriosclerotic brain disease. However, these symptoms can also result from other, perhaps functional, causes; at the same time, chronic brain syndrome can occur unaccompanied by any extreme functional change (Simon, 1971).

In some instances, symptoms that initially appear to indicate a serious organic brain change actually represent a nutritional deficit, and the patient's confusion and other symptoms cease as soon as proper diet is initiated. The diets of the elderly poor are often not adequate for proper physical or mental health, and some who are not especially poor suffer from nutritional deficits caused by improper eating habits.

Other emotional problems also involve the elderly. Alcoholism, for example, although less common among the elderly than among younger age groups, remains a problem; suicide rates tend to increase rapidly after the sixties, and the proportion of suicide attempts that do not eventuate in death diminishes drastically, suggesting that the elderly suicide is not calling for help but sincerely intends to die. Suicide rates increase for men and decrease for women after middle age.

Functional psychosis is more difficult to evaluate. Some elderly patients who have been hospitalized for many years, perhaps decades, seem to "burn out": their more obvious symptoms disappear. Nonetheless, about half of those hospitalized who are between 65 and 74, and nearly 40% of those 75 and older, were diagnosed as having functional psychoses (1963 statistics) (Simon, 1971). Considering the multiple losses that the elderly suffer—friends and family, functional performance, social roles—it is not surprising that many are emotionally disturbed. The real emotional-disturbance rate among the elderly may be higher than the official rate, since many people will tolerate behavior in an older person that would send them rushing to the authorities if the same behavior occurred in a younger person.

Some Final Comments

Individual differences among the elderly seem so great that trends in personality development and change are very difficult to discern. The definition of "successful" aging is even more uncertain, since the very notion of what is successful varies from person to person. It makes sense to assume that life satisfaction in the later years results from some interaction among one's earlier life, one's expectations of the later years, one's personality, and situational factors. The person's physical and medical conditions also play a part.

The issue of interventions necessarily arises. Is there anything I can do as a young or middle-aged person that will affect my self-esteem and self-concept when I am elderly? Is there anything I can do, as an individual concerned with those who are now old, that will affect their self-esteem and self-concept? Intervening in the life of another person should not be done lightly; many interventions—even well-meaning ones—backfire, and others have unexpected and undesirable side effects. Moreover, many people resent the idea that someone else is planning to intervene in their lives.

Perhaps successful aging in an individual may be encouraged by his learning something about what it means to become elderly, particularly in regard to effective methods of coping with changes, so that he can live as much as possible as he wishes. The needs of the elderly are basically the same as the needs of other age groups: first, older people need to have their physiological and safety needs satisfied; second, they need to feel they are loved so that they can maintain self-esteem. And the elderly—just like all others—need to be challenged and need to be able to realize their own potential. To fulfill these needs, they require both sensory and cognitive stimulation, although the specific activities stimulating to the elderly may differ from those preferred by younger people.

Much of the life situation of the elderly seems to conspire against their having an adequate self-concept: work and family roles often diminish in importance, income and social status are not as high, strength is lost, and ability to do many kinds of tasks is reduced. Yet the need for dignity is just as important in old age as in youth, just as important in the dying process as in the rest of life.

Chapter Four

Relating to Others

Nothing is forever. From the time you are conceived until after your death, you are in a state of dynamic change. Some changes result primarily from processes going on within the organism; some evolve largely as the result of relationships with other organisms. And these two forces, the internal and the interpersonal, interact with each other. As you become older, you change in size, appearance, awareness of the world, intellectual capacity, sexual drives, and innumerable other ways. As you undergo change, the perceptions others have of you undergo similar (although not necessarily congruous) change.

Moreover, the others who are perceiving you are themselves undergoing change. Your parents change from people who control you to people with whom you can interact on some basis of equality to people you may have to care for. Your children change from weak, helpless infants to independent adults. Brothers and sisters, teachers and clergymen, neighbors and friends, and employers, coworkers, and employees are all changing. A permanent relationship with someone of the opposite sex (and occasionally of the same sex) is established. It grows, changes its course many times, and is eventually broken by death, by separation, or by psychological withdrawal.

Nothing is forever.

Attitudes Toward Aging and the Elderly

Each individual performs many roles that are normally a lifetime affair: sex, ethnicity, national origin. He also has other kinds of status over which he has some degree of selective power: education, vocation, neighborhood. One's age status is not a lifetime matter, but neither does the individual have any control over his age status (although he need not always act in accordance with the standards implicitly established for his age group).

There is obviously some discrepancy between what it is actually like to be old and what any given individual or group of individuals believe it is like to be old. Nonetheless, elderly people's perceptions of their roles not only reflect reality to an appreciable extent, but they also create reality. If young people believe that old people are lonely, the young will behave in terms of this perception: they may attempt to befriend the elderly, or they may develop an intense fear of aging themselves, which can cause them to avoid older people.

Although the research on altered patterns of self-esteem as a function of age has not provided consistent results, studies of attitudes toward aging and the elderly are quite consistent. Whether the sample responding is young, middle-aged, or old, all the research indicates that being old is considered less desirable than being young, although elderly respondents are more positive in their evaluations of old age than are people of younger ages. In a study of young, middle-aged, and older adults, all three age groups stated that the death of a 75-year-old was less tragic than the death of a person at any other age (Kalish & Reynolds, 1975).

Old Age as Perceived by Children and Youth

When over 200 third-graders were asked to write about "an old person," it became immediately obvious that character differentiations among adult age groups are readily made, even at this age. The most common response made by these children was that older persons are "kind": over 75% included that appraisal in their sentences. Interestingly, the second most common evaluation was that older persons are "mean": 25% of the children included that statement. (The analysis permitted each child's paper to be scored for more than one category, and sometimes a child would mention both "kind" and "mean" characteristics.) Loneliness, having leisure time, and eccentricities (often interpreted as senile behavior) were all touched upon by 10% or more of the children. Although fewer children described old people's physical characteristics, walking problems and general feebleness were each mentioned by about 15% of the group (Hickey, Hickey, & Kalish, 1968).

To show the perceptiveness of some of the children, I will list a few of their comments.

> My sister and I like to walk down to the corner with old Mr. Smith, but we have to walk slower when we are with him.
> They always ask you to talk louder.
> Old people usually die, or lose a leg or an arm.

Old people are mean, and they don't let you walk on their lawn.
Old people are funny [p. 224].

Although the third-graders appeared both aware of the conditions of old age and reasonably favorably disposed toward older people, a follow-up study found that older children held less positive views, and high school and college students still less positive views (Hickey & Kalish, 1968). An earlier study of high school and college students had shown their image of the elderly to be unpleasant and without significant positive values (Kastenbaum & Durkee, 1964). In the past few years, however, a great many articles and television presentations have depicted the elderly in a sympathetic fashion. Furthermore, attention has been focused on the difficulties faced by low-income persons (as so many of the elderly are) throughout the United States and Canada. It is likely that young people now have a greater understanding of and sympathy for the elderly than they had a decade ago.

Old Age as Perceived by Adults

It is common contention that the elderly are especially disliked and that getting old is especially threatening in contemporary Western societies, whereas less developed nations, as did the Western nations in past centuries, accord higher status to the aging. Although this evaluation may be true, the evidence is shaky (see McTavish, 1971, for an excellent brief review of the evidence). The elderly apparently receive the greatest respect in societies that permit them to retain the greatest amount of economic and political power (Simmons, 1945). These areas of the world also tend to be autocratic in their form of government. In the United States and Canada, very few young and middle-aged people can be manipulated into caring for their parents in order to ensure that they inherit their parents' estate; whatever respect and caring they display toward their parents result from some combination of community pressure, their sense of obligation and duty, and their personal affection. In many other parts of the world, however, the old person retains control of his land or business, and the only way his children can receive a share is to acknowledge his authority. Respect for the aged is apparently highest in these societies. This fact suggests that greater respect will be accorded the elderly in Western nations if the elderly become more powerful (an unlikely possibility) or if their economic position improves. For example, the elderly in low-income Western families retain some economic leverage. Many low-income families are willing to keep their elderly at home, not only out of personal affection or loyalty but out of necessity: the Social Security or welfare check of the old person is a much-needed contribution to the family budget.

Having reviewed several dozen studies of attitudes toward the elderly, McTavish (1971) lists the stereotypes emerging from these investigations: ill, tired, uninterested in sex, mentally slower, forgetful, less able to learn new things, grouchy, withdrawn, self-pitying, less likely to participate in activities (with the exception, perhaps, of religion), isolated, living in the least happy and least fortunate time of life, unproductive, and defensive (p. 97). McTavish concludes that, in spite of these stereotypes, attitudes toward the elderly are not consistently negative and are often related to other variables; higher education and higher social class in the elderly, for example, are predictive of favorable attitudes.

How, then, do the self-perceptions of the elderly relate to the perceptions that other generations have of them? In approaching this issue, Ahammer and Baltes (1972) asked respondents representing three age groups (adolescent, adult, and elderly) to evaluate the desirability of specified behaviors from their own point of view and from the points of view of the other two generations. The behaviors were categorized in terms of the personality dimensions of affiliation, achievement, autonomy, and nurturance. Both the adolescents and the adults perceived the elderly as placing greater value on nurturing behavior and less value on autonomous behavior than the elderly actually did. These results suggest that the elderly are less willing to give up their freedom and to play a nurturing role than the middle-aged and teen-agers assume. A picture emerges: the elderly are being told, in essence, "take it easy; be a little passive and be loving, like grandparents should be," whereas the elderly resist being molded into this structure.

In a study of three generations of women in one family (Kalish & Johnson, 1972), Ann Johnson and I found that the middle generation, the mothers, were more negatively disposed toward older people and more fearful of the aging process than were either the daughters or the grandmothers, and that the grandmothers expressed the most favorable feelings toward aging and the aged. We speculated that middle-generation women often found themselves caring for aged parents while simultaneously noticing undesirable signs of aging in themselves. Also, mother-daughter tensions would often direct one generation toward resenting the preceding generation, perhaps also helping to promote affinity with the nonadjacent generation.

Another finding that intrigued us was the relationship of political views to attitudes toward old people and toward one's own aging. We found that, among the mothers and grandmothers, no relationship existed between political liberalism and attitudes toward aging. However, with the college-student generation, the women with more liberal beliefs were more negatively disposed toward aging and the aged. Presumably, these college women perceived the elderly as a conservative political force that impeded their pursuit of their political goals (if liberal) or supported their political views (if conservative).

Implications of Age-ism

[Positive] Attitudes toward aging may be critical for adjustment and survival. It is possible that attitudes contribute to observed maladaptive behaviors among the aged, some of which may result in premature death. Negative views of aging, life in general, and oneself may result in an old person's unwillingness or inability to seek needed services, health care, or other types of assistance. Negative attitudes of old people may affect others in their environs, who in turn may feel free to respond negatively to old people or to ignore them completely [Bennett & Eckman, 1973, p. 575].

These statements are hypotheses, not established facts. They may not fairly describe the overall picture. Yet there is a strong ring of truth in these statements. Even though research data do not, for example, show a reduction in the self-rated self-esteem of older persons, there is little doubt that the self-esteem of many older persons drops as a result of the process of aging and—even more—as a result of some of the disruptive forces, discussed earlier, that accompany aging in disproportionate numbers.

One obvious example of age-ism—those negative attitudes toward the aged mentioned by Bennett and Eckman—that influences the survival of the elderly is the attitudes of health practitioners. Geriatric medicine, geriatric social welfare, continuing education for the elderly, psychotherapeutic services for the elderly—none of these specialized services has had an overabundance of ready recruits. Health practitioners in general seem to assign lower priority to service to the elderly than to service to any other age group.

No wonder many people resent growing old. Not only do the elderly frequently suffer significant losses in psychomotor skills, in visual and auditory sensitivity, in income, and in work opportunities, but they must deal with the essentially negative and often patronizing attitudes of younger people—which undoubtedly are partial reflections of the attitudes of the elderly themselves. Older persons perceive their own declining status and, sometimes, declining abilities, and they also must begin to recognize that their personal future is limited by imminent death. Since they serve to remind others of aging and death, their very presence is often upsetting, eliciting responses from younger people that range from condescending humor to bitter anger; many of us resent having to contemplate our own finitude. Recognizing what is happening to them, feeling anger and resentment and helplessness, many elderly people fight back in the only way available to the powerless: they complain, nag, criticize, become irritable and petulant, and alternate between assertions of independence and obvious manipulations to permit dependence.

This picture is often true of unhappy elderly people. The fascinating contradiction is that so many of the elderly, even those who are financially impoverished, continue to report high life satisfaction and high morale.

Society's Values

Given the fact that the latter decades of life are valued less than the earlier years, what does this say about the priority system applied to human values in Western nations? Why do we value the elderly less than their youthful successors? In response to these rhetorical questions, let me hazard a list of what I perceive to be those characteristics and conditions most respected by people in Western nations.

> achievement and potential for achievement
> productivity of goods, services, or artistic endeavors
> ability to carry on human relationships successfully
> independence and self-sufficiency
> past accomplishments
> ability to enjoy life
> knowledge and awareness, capacity for grasping technology
> physical attractiveness, sexual capacity, and physical vitality
> influence and power
> material wealth
> ability to provide nurturance to others
> wisdom
> desire to invest time, energy, and money in the future

You may believe that some of these values are misperceived, and you personally may not accept many of them, but you are likely to accept the list as at least representative of the way we invest our time, money, and energies. On only two characteristics listed here are the elderly likely to hold their own: past accomplishments and wisdom. Even these are questionable: past accomplishments often dwindle in importance as the years go by, and records are always being broken. Being the first man with the company to sell 5 million dollars' worth of insurance, the woman who worked as a physician in a rural community for 45 years, the sergeant whose World War II unit destroyed the most German gun emplacements—these accomplishments mean less and less to most people as time passes. To attribute wisdom to the aged is also questionable, since views and values considered wise at one time may soon be considered outdated. It is true that the elderly have had immeasurable experience, but much of their experience was gained during a time when different values were in vogue. For example, our relatively new awareness of environmental pollution in its myriad forms has, by itself, immensely affected our general perceptions of the wisdom of economic growth.

In essence, then, the older person does not fare well when evaluated against the major criteria that our culture implicitly sets up. Let me suggest a few alternative criteria that we might specify.

> adherence to traditional codes of Judeo-Christian morality
> maintenance of one marriage throughout a long life
> willingness to defend one's country in a defensive war or to support one's country in a controversial involvement—or even to give one's life for it
> having a large number of descendants
> having experienced wars and depressions

This list is hardly a recitation of our national value system today. Earlier in our history, many of the values on the second list would have been on the first, and many of the items on the first list probably did not discriminate so effectively against the elderly. For example, in a rural, nonindustrial society, knowledge and technological awareness are found in the older, not in the younger, members; the senior generation retains greater control over land and business, thus controlling entrée to jobs and financial resources.

Whoever wishes to intervene in the process by which the elderly find themselves less useful to society must consider how to change society's —or at least his own—basic values; and this is one of the most difficult goals a person can set for himself.

The Older Person's Family

The older person, like anyone else, has many family roles. He or she is parent, spouse, aunt or uncle, cousin, brother or sister, and, occasionally, the child of living parents. (In one instance, a father and his son were in the same geriatric institution; their respective ages were 94 and 71.) Of course, elderly persons are much more likely to be grandparents than younger persons (although 35-year-old grandparents are not unheard of), and they are often great-grandparents. Occasionally, even a five-generation family is found.

As is true of other adult age groups, most older persons in the United States are married (71% of the men and 37% of the women), and most of them have living children (80% of the men and 76% of the women). As is not true of other age groups, large numbers of the elderly are widows

(52%) or widowers (19%). Although many older persons have lost a spouse through death, some have subsequently remarried, and others have been widowed or widowered more than once (USDHEW, 1971). Therefore, the figures underestimate the extent of such losses suffered by the elderly. Bereavement may be one of the most crucial concerns of the elderly and of those who are involved with them, either professionally or personally (Shanas, 1962).

Two ideas that many Americans seem to cherish today is that three generations of the same family were more likely to share a household in the past than they are in the present, and that today the generations are alienated from each other. But the available data contradict this notion. Multigenerational families in the same household appear to be no less common today than they were a century ago (Beresford & Rivlin, 1969), amounting to about 8% of all American families (Troll, 1971). Unfortunately, these figures refer only to the quantity and not to the quality of intrafamily relationships. In the United States, the multigenerational family seems to develop primarily when the nuclear family is disrupted by death or divorce (Beresford & Rivlin, 1969), but financial expediency or child-care needs may also encourage such living arrangements. In fact, older people usually desire to live independently of their children for as long as they possibly can, not only to avoid impinging upon the freedom of the younger people but also to retain their own sense of competence and their privacy, independence, and self-determination. Research on this issue is quite consistent (Troll, 1971).

The Nature of Family Relationships

By the time they reach age 65, most people are living either alone or with only their spouses. In the United States, nearly 80% of older men and nearly 60% of older women live in a family unit, most often consisting of husband and wife. If the husband is still alive after 65, the chances are nine out of ten that he is technically considered the head of household, although occasionally another relative is defined as head. Fewer elderly people lived with their children in 1970 than in previous census years, even though this independence often had to be purchased at considerable financial sacrifice (Brotman, 1972).

The impact of changing family relationships on people in their later years cannot be seen in statistics alone. The entire nature of a person's family role undergoes change. For example, in the early and middle years of parenthood, the mother and father provide emotional, social, and financial support for their children. In the later years, a role reversal often occurs: middle-aged children become increasingly responsible for providing various kinds of support for their parents and, less often, for other older persons. An analysis of three adult generations within the same family showed that the grandparents received more support than they gave in terms of economic help, emotional gratification, care in times of illness, and help with household management. At the same time, they gave more help with child care than they received, not an especially startling finding (Hill, 1965). However, Troll (1971) suggests that social-class differences in these support patterns may be important: the middle-class elderly tend to give help to their children until much later in their children's lives, whereas the working-class elderly are more likely to receive help from their children. Middle-class parents are also more likely to give their children money, whereas working-class parents are more likely to give them services.

There is also considerable debate on the concept of role reversal. Blenkner (1965) believes that *filial maturity* is a better term, signifying that adult children, as they reach their own middle years, should be able to permit their parents to depend on them. The roles, therefore, are not seen as reversed; instead, changing roles are seen as a natural outcome of the increasing maturity of adult children and their acceptance of what is expected of them.

Another study found that nearly two-thirds of the elderly individuals surveyed had seen at least one of their children during the 24 hours prior to the interview, and that a great majority lived within 30 minutes' driving time of at least one child (Shanas et al., 1968b). Other investigations add support to the notion that adult children visit and, when it is necessary, care for their elderly parents (Streib, 1958; Sussman, 1965). The services each generation offers the other are a function of income, health, family relationships, needs, and family status. For example, grandparents are more likely to provide baby-sitting help and more likely to give money and valuable gifts when their grandchildren are young, when they themselves are healthy, and when finances are not a major problem. Help during periods of illness is often exchanged; presumably, the elderly person receives more and gives less as he ages. In general, parents and their adult children maintain an active exchange of money, gifts, help, and advice.

Family responsibility in the United States and Canada is perceived essentially as serial rather than reciprocal. That is, each generation is seen as primarily responsible for the support of the succeeding generation. Parents, during the years when they are most capable, are expected to care for their children, but when parents become less capable and their children more so, the children—now adults—are expected to attend to their own children first and to their parents second.

Many older persons state—and most, I'm certain, are sincere when they do—that they do not wish to be a burden upon their children. Their statement is consistent with the national value of retaining one's independence. I have sometimes asked these older people—or middle-aged people, when they make the same statement—to consider why they were so willing to accept their children as burdens for so many years but are now unwilling to be the recipients of equivalent support. (See p. 85 for fuller discussion of independence/dependence.) In spite of the prevailing value of serial responsibility, and in spite of the innumerable well-documented stories of children who refuse to provide financial or emotional support to elderly parents, many gerontologists—myself included—believe that the elderly are not nearly so maltreated by their children as is often supposed.

Nonetheless, the quality of the interaction between adult child and elderly parent is at least as important to life satisfaction for the parent as the quantity of contacts between them (Rosow, 1967). Unfortunately, the nature of quality is more difficult to understand; we can't count it, as we can count the frequency of contacts, and we often need to be dubious about what people tell us, since they may be motivated to have the situation appear either better or worse than it actually is.

Neither should we jump too quickly to the conclusion that children are simply ungrateful if they do not offer their parents proper care. In many cases, for example, there has been a long history of estrangement between parent and child. Since our society does not invoke severe sanctions against children who ignore their parents, support of the elderly tends to be based either on feelings of love and affection or on a sense of obligation and duty —or on both. The middle-aged child is often caught between feelings of obligation to his own children, spouse, and work and feelings of obligation to his parents. Elderly parents themselves frequently insist that a grandchild attend college even when it means a loss of financial support from their children.

Another ramification is that a middle-aged couple is much more likely today to have one or more parents to be concerned with, whereas in times past relatively few people lived long enough to become dependent in their old age. I would also hazard that our society's present emphasis on self-actualization and personal growth, as opposed to emphasis on obligation to the support of others, tends to draw many people away from making major sacrifices for the elderly. But selfless as well as selfish adult children do exist: the problem is too often seen only from the viewpoint of one generation or the other. Relationships between the generations are obviously a complex matter, not helped at all by creating villains of the elderly (for being difficult to relate to) or of the adult children (for being ungrateful).

Sex differences complicate the situation still further. Adult male children appear to receive more financial aid from their parents, whereas daughters receive more services (Sussman, 1953). At the same time, married daughters seem to maintain closer ties with their parents than do married sons, and greater conflict may occur between daughters and their mothers-in-law, perhaps resulting from their competition for the role of providing emotional support for the man (Sussman, 1965). An overall tendency exists for a middle-aged couple to be closer to the wife's family than to the husband's family (Troll, 1971). An intriguing question arises: how will the increasing tendency toward egalitarian sex roles, and the increasing number of women who work outside the home, influence such relationships?

Grandparenthood

One family role that has received virtually no attention until recently is the role of grandparent. This neglect seems especially odd in light of the fact that more and more people now live to be grandparents or even great-grandparents. Furthermore, "more grandchildren have an association with a grandparent now than ... in 1900" (Nimkoff, 1961, p. 735). This statement is true both because of increased longevity and because many residents of the United States and Canada at the turn of the century had left elderly parents behind in Europe or elsewhere, and their children simply never saw their grandparents. Today, 70% of people over 65 have living grandchildren (Atchley, 1972).

But there are deeper reasons why we should be concerned with understanding the grandparent role. Being a grandparent may take on special meaning to the elderly as other areas of role-performance become closed to them. Furthermore, grandparents can have satisfying contacts with grandchildren that involve a minimum of obligation and responsibility, so that both can be freer and less guarded in the relationship than parents and children can be. Interactions between grandparents and grandchildren include (1) both brief and extended visits, (2) exchange of gifts, (3) exchange of letters and other communications, and (4) the exchange of experience; the grandparents can follow the growth, development, and adventures of the young, and the children can share the wisdom and experience of the elderly (Smith, 1965).

Styles of grandparenting have also been described; three are especially relevant (Neugarten & Weinstein, 1964). (1) The *formal* grandparent likes to give presents and treats to his grandchildren and occasionally likes to baby-sit or provide other services, but he essentially prefers to avoid intruding on the parental role. (2) The *fun-seeker* participates in an informal, often playful, relationship with his grandchildren. He emphasizes mutual enjoyment and mutual participation rather than assuming an authoritarian role. (3) The *distant* grandparent has infrequent contact with grandchildren and likes to remain remote, although he gives occasional gifts.

Style of grandparenting results from a number of different factors. Two obvious ones are the personalities of grandparent and grandchild and the frequency and quality of interactions between them. The geographical distance between them, the ways in which the parents structure the child's time and availability, and adequacy of income and transportation are all major determinants. The age of the grandparent also makes a significant difference (Neugarten & Weinstein, 1964). So does the age of the grandchild. One observer, although basing her interpretation on only 15 semistructured interviews, suggested that many grandparents could be classified as "fun-seeking" when the grandchildren are young but become more formal as the needs of the grandchildren change with their greater maturity, a change that grandparents sometimes accept only with regret (Hubert, 1970). Grandparents seem more able to enjoy being with grandchildren who are young than with those who are in later childhood or adolescence (Kahana & Coe, 1969).

For some grandparents, their role gives them a sense of biological renewal or continuity—a sense of immortality through their grandchildren; others see their role as a means of emotional self-fulfillment, vicarious accomplishment (what they and their children could not achieve, their grandchildren might), and satisfaction as a resource person or teacher (Neugarten & Weinstein, 1964).

Grandparents serve another kind of function, one not often considered even by those most intimately involved. Young children observe the ways in which their parents relate to their grandparents. Although no research has been done (to my knowledge) in this area, it would be interesting to learn whether the reaction of adult children to their elderly parents is in any way reflected when those adult children become elderly and their children must work out ways of relating to them.

Sometimes an affinity is noted between grandchildren in their teens or early twenties and their grandparents. Perhaps each can relate to the other without the tensions that exist between parent and child. Their closeness might be due in part to the circumstances that the young and the old share. Both are (1) age groups adjacent to the age group that dominates society, but neither has much power or much influence on the decision-makers; (2) constantly reminded of their nonproductive roles (at least the retired elderly and the not-yet-working young), and both see themselves as taking from society without putting anything back in, although the potential of the young to be productive in the future is denied the old; (3) seen as having a life filled with leisure: education and retirement are seen as pleasure, not as work or boredom; (4) living with their time relatively unstructured—the time structure that does exist for them is not perceived by the middle-aged; (5) thought to be inadequately educated—the young are not yet educated by experience and the old often lack formal education; (6)

poor and therefore vulnerable and therefore weak. In spite of these similarities, however, we know that there are tensions between the young and the old, based in large part upon the differing needs and values of the two age groups.

Husbands and Wives

The marital relationship is one of the most important—perhaps the most important—relationship experienced in the adult years. Older couples, at least according to data collected about two decades ago (1957), reported the same degrees of marital happiness and the same frequency of feelings of inadequacy as did other age groups, but they were less likely to report marital problems (Gurin, Veroff, & Feld, 1960).

During retirement, the husband spends much more of his time at home. Marital relationships that were sustained largely because the man and woman were busy and could avoid encountering each other may become stressful. One woman expressed it succinctly: "I married him for better or for worse, but not for lunch." In marriages that are at least moderately happy, the couple do more things together—traveling, visits to their children, social activities, and housework or shopping (Lipman, 1962). The role of the husband tends to shift from that of provider to that of helper, and the role of the wife demands a greater amount of love and understanding than before (Troll, 1971).

Divorce is still infrequent in this age group, but it appears to be increasing fairly rapidly. The divorce rate for persons who had been married for 25 to 29 years rose by 36% between 1963 and 1967 (USDHEW, 1971). Perhaps a combination of less punitive divorce laws and less community disapproval of divorce has permitted older people greater freedom to dissolve unhappy marriages. An alternative hypothesis is that marriage, even marriage with a 35- to 50-year history, is simply less satisfying today than in times past. Another possibility is that people are increasingly unable to maintain a commitment to permanent relationships.

Remarriage, however, is quite common in this age group. Studying 100 retirement marriages, McKain (1968) concludes that companionship is the most important basis for remarriage late in life. He states that meaning and purpose in life can be enhanced by a good marital relationship, and that these are often lacking among older people who live alone. Sexual satisfaction was identified as another important reason for remarriage. It should be noted that, in this study, the concept of sex embraced more than intercourse and included many kinds of physical touching and emotional responsiveness. Financial and health reasons for remarriage were also given.

Loss of Family Roles

One major role-loss that takes place relatively early in life is assumed to be especially cogent for women. Whether it is indeed a major loss and whether men are immune to its effects are both unsettled issues. The "empty nest" syndrome, which may appear when parents find that their children are established on their own and have much less need of their supervision and even of their emotional support, is often cited as a reason for emotional upset in middle-aged women. Often coinciding with the menopause, this period is often found to be filled with stress. This theory has never, however, been fully substantiated. In fact, many women (and their husbands) in their late middle years express a sense of relief when their children no longer impinge so much upon their time and energies (and budget). Of course, these comments should not imply that no women are susceptible to the syndrome.

Women tend to marry men older than themselves, and women live longer than men, at least in developed nations. These two well-known factors combine to create a vastly larger number of widows than widowers. Among women over 65, far more are widowed than are married, a statistic that suggests how pervasive this problem is.

The most serious form of loss of family role occurs through the death of a family member, especially a spouse. "The cultural evolution that has made marriage an integral part of our social organization has done little to ensure that the functions that it performs will be adequately carried out after its dissolution" (Parkes, 1972, p. 8). As a result, the surviving widow or widower suffers not only the grief arising from the loss but also the deprivation that comes with the spouse's absence. Loneliness, lack of someone with whom to share affection and work tasks, and loss of sexual satisfactions are some of the deprivations that accompany the death of a spouse (Parkes, 1972). It is possible to find substitute relationships that alleviate the sense of deprivation without reducing the sense of loss and grief. Conversely, some survivors may never experience grief—and may even be somewhat pleased that an encumbering unhappy relationship has ceased—but may still feel deprived by the absence of the not-especially-loved dead person.

Stigmatization, as well as loss and deprivation, is often felt by a surviving spouse. The role-expectations of an elderly unmarried person are quite different from those of an elderly married person or from those of a younger unmarried person. Friendship patterns change; adult children begin to talk of combining households (or at least they worry about it); the elderly person's motivation to cook good meals, to retain good grooming practices, and to keep a neat house may diminish. While the widow or widower often disengages, at least temporarily, from the social milieu, people in the environment seem to disengage from him even more, as though the widow or widower were stigmatized. Companionship, except with others of the same status, is often difficult to find. ". . . People . . . previously friendly and approachable become embarrassed and strained" in the bereaved person's presence (Parkes, 1972, p. 8).

Older widows do not appear to share the significant increase in incidence of physical illness that younger widows undergo shortly after their bereavement. This fact may be partially explained by the phenomenon termed "rehearsal for widowhood." This syndrome can begin in the middle or even in the younger years. The woman begins to anticipate what her life will be like when and if she is later widowed. In this way, she can work through some of the emotional problems of widowhood before the actual occurrence. Elderly women, of course, have lived through more deaths of others and have probably rehearsed more extensively for widowhood. (Men undoubtedly experience a comparable phenomenon, but I believe that it occurs less frequently and with less intensity.)

Bereavement requires that the elderly survivor abandon old assumptions about the world and begin to live with new ones. This transition can be difficult, and the survivor often feels the deceased person to be "still very close" or thinks of the dead "as though he were still alive and with me." Visiting with the dead in dreams, sensing the person's presence, or experiencing seeing, hearing, or touching the dead are not uncommon (Parkes, 1970).

Whereas the older widow has a wide potential group of other widows to whom she can reach out for companionship, the older widower has relatively few male friends, although he is likely to feel somewhat compensated for this lack by the many widows available for social—and often sexual—relationships. The bereavement of the surviving husband can also be more disruptive than that of the surviving wife, since it requires him to undertake household tasks for which his previous experience and self-image probably did not prepare him (Berardo, 1970). Once again, we will eventually have the chance to see whether egalitarian marriages will alter the patterns of adjustment of the elderly to loss of a spouse.

An extremely useful program for recently bereaved widows, called the Widow-to-Widow program (although other names may be used in local communities), has recently been established. Women who have had a very recent bereavement are contacted by other widows who have been able to recover reasonably well from their own grief. Widows who work with the program are given considerable training, but they have rarely received professional degrees or had counseling experience before being widowed. Because help is coming from someone who has shared the same experience, the recipient will be less likely to feel "crazy" or incompetent. This program is spreading around the country as one part of the movement that has seen innumerable groups established, by persons who have gone through a particular crisis, to help those going through a similar crisis (Silverman, 1972).

Independence and Dependence

One of the recurring themes in the writings of gerontologists is dependency. Independence and mastery of oneself and one's environment are basic values to most Americans. To be dependent is to be weak and vulnerable, to have to give up a certain amount of power over your own life, to be unable to make certain important decisions, and to be in what is commonly called a "one-down" position.

The concept of dependency, as applied to the elderly, is really a grouping of separate concepts. For example, we can consider dependency in terms of an interpersonal relationship in which one person gives and another receives. Or dependency can refer to a quality or condition of the individual, implying that some incapacity in the individual produces the need for help. A blind person, for instance, depends upon others, even though he may not have any dependency relationships, or dependency can be approached as a relatively enduring personality characteristic. Finally, dependency can be seen as residing in human behavior rather than in relationships, in a given condition, or in the personality (Kalish, 1969b).

An older person (or, indeed, a person of any age) often attempts to manipulate someone he perceives as stronger than himself, with the aim of obtaining a protector who will relieve tension and anxiety, offer satisfactions, and help him to cope with an environment that is seen as threatening (Goldfarb, 1969). When such a person is found, or when these needs are satisfied in some fashion, stress is reduced and feelings of anxiety subside. One psychiatrist reduced the number of telephone calls and visits to a hospital clinic from elderly people with dubious medical complaints by simply being available when they wanted him, regardless of whether they had any real medical problem. Once the elderly people found that a stronger person was available to give them help when they really needed it, they no longer felt that they had to express their dependency needs through constant clinic visits (Lipsitt, 1969).

Four kinds of normal dependency in aging have been listed. (1) Economic dependency occurs when the older person is no longer a wage earner but must depend on some combination of retirement and Social Security payments, welfare, and family gifts. (2) Physical dependency arises when the person's biological functions suffer decrements and no longer permit him to perform necessary tasks such as walking, shopping, visiting others, or preparing food. (3) Mental dependency parallels physical dependency; it occurs when deterioration or change in the central nervous system produces marked deficits in memory, orientation, comprehension, or judgment. (4) Social dependency arises with the loss of meaningful others in the elderly person's life. It produces a reduced awareness of the larger society, reduced individual power, and limitations on social roles (Blenkner, 1969).

Although the elderly individual will often work out the solution to his dependency needs by himself or within his kinship group, the society at large is sometimes required to help with one or more of the needs listed above (Blenkner, 1969). And, since help with one kind of dependency tends to alleviate problems with the other kinds of dependency, such outside help can have a salutary effect. For example, helping a person meet his physical needs may enable him to feel less anxious, to regain his former cognitive performance level, and to interact with others and cope with social dependency needs.

Dependence, however, need not be approached as an evil. It should also be differentiated from submissiveness. A submissive person does what others tell him without making demands, but a dependent person—by virtue of the mere state of being dependent—requires that people relate to him. An old person who is dependent is often seen as a nuisance. Physicians, social workers, and adult children often resent the elderly's dependency on them.

Many of the elderly deeply resent their own dependency. They would rather retain mastery over their environment than have to call on others for help. Ironically, their resentment of their condition can cause them to complain, to worry, and then—for fear of losing their necessary relationships with others—to become yet more dependent.

Not all cultures place so much emphasis on independence, although this value is found in varying degrees in major Western cultures. The Igbo of Africa, for example, are quite different. "The Igbo elder is no more productive in his advanced years, but he can demand care as a publicly acknowledged right without any sense of guilt, ego damage, or loss of face. Whoever fails to give such care is subject to public scorn and ridicule, cut off not only from the spiritual benefits of the ancestors but also from the material benefits of the system" (Shelton, 1969, p. 104).

Friends and Neighbors

A frequent source of disagreement among gerontologists and others concerned with the elderly is whether older persons prefer friendships with others roughly their own age, or whether they will gain more satisfaction from having friends whose ages are spread fairly evenly across the entire age distribution. I tend to agree with Rosow when he states that "there is an effective social barrier between the generations which propinquity and contact apparently do not dispel" (1967, p. 34). Even when young and old live near each other and have contact with each other, friendships do not often emerge. I do not say that they never emerge or that no older person prefers social interactions with young people. You can ask yourself what proportion of your available leisure time you would wish to spend with people ten years younger than yourself (if you are under 30) or 15 years younger (if you are over 30).

Perhaps older people feel most comfortable with their age peers because they feel excluded and unwanted in groups of younger people; or perhaps they feel more at home with people who have shared their life spans, memories, and—probably most important—period of early socialization. They share recollections of the same ballplayers, movie actors, automobiles, and politicians; they remember dancing the same dances, using the same slang, fighting in the same wars, wearing the same clothing styles. People who share common racial, linguistic, religious, or national backgrounds often cluster together; age is simply one more basis for such clustering.

A careful study of older apartment-dwellers in Cleveland, Ohio, showed that those living in buildings with a high percentage of older persons (50% or more of the households had at least one member over 65) had more friends than those living in buildings with relatively few elderly people (Rosow, 1967). The working-class elderly in this survey tended to draw more of their friends from the immediate neighborhood than did the middle-class elderly, and, therefore, living in close proximity to other elderly people was even more important for them.

To the extent to which preference for age peers results from feeling victimized by prejudice and discrimination on the part of the young, program planners may wish to contemplate ways to intervene. To the extent to which this preference reflects a sincere desire to remain with one's reference group, program planners should probably avoid interfering. The problem is to determine the relative impact of each of these pressures. Most gerontologists prefer the idea of providing the elderly with as many options as possible and then permitting each individual to make his own decision.

Simply counting the number of friends a person claims to have or the number of visits he makes to neighbors is not a sufficient measure of his effective social integration in his community. Such social integration is based on three dimensions: values, formal and informal group memberships, and social roles. ". . . People are tied into their society essentially through their beliefs, the groups that they belong to, and the positions that they occupy" (Rosow, 1967, p. 9).

Data from another context support Rosow's position. In studying the ability to cope with the social and emotional stresses found among the elderly, researchers found that the availability of a close friend or confidant often differentiated those who were coping effectively from those who were not (Lowenthal & Haven, 1968).

When older people are relocated to new neighborhoods because of urban renewal or other factors, their social integration is diminished or destroyed—sometimes only temporarily, but often permanently. Although they may find new friends and confidants, this takes time. Also, they frequently find that housing in the new neighborhoods is some distance away from friends, distance that affects their network of social relationships. Of course, when an elderly person leaves his community to live with his adult children or to enter a long-term care facility, the same disruptions occur. His inter-relationships with his family or his new relationships formed within the institution occasionally replace his old ties, but in many instances he never finds substitutes.

Aging and Ethnicity

We all belong to one or more ethnic groups, but not all ethnic-group memberships are equally salient or meaningful. When the older American is black, Latin American, Native American, or Asian American, or belongs to another of the non-Anglo groups, his ethnicity is likely to be extremely salient. For many people, identification with white ethnic groups is equally significant.

Let's examine one example.

When a black American becomes old, he often finds that he receives attention both from younger blacks and from those interested in the elderly in general. Each of these groups believes that they "understand" the older black because they share so much with him. Both are often wrong. If young and middle-aged whites do not understand older whites, there is no reason to believe that young and middle-aged blacks understand the elderly of their own race any better. Conversely, if whites often lack understanding of blacks in general, there is no reason to believe that whites involved with the elderly would understand elderly black people any better.

Only in recent years has there been any research or writing on older persons of minority groups. Elderly blacks are often considered to be in multiple jeopardy because they are old, black, and (often) poor. Any one of these characteristics requires special efforts to cope within society; all three in combination place great demands on one's coping skills. And the 1970 census counted 809,000 black women and 608,000 black men over 65 in the United States.

Just as I began this book by insisting that "older people" are not a single entity, although we often discuss them as if they were, "older members of an ethnic group" are not a single entity. The elderly black woman living in rural Alabama has a life much different from that of the elderly black woman who came to Detroit during World War II and stayed there. The elderly Mexican American farmer in New Mexico, whose family settled there in 1820, shares some experiences with the elderly Mexican American who is a migratory worker, or with the Mexican American Catholic priest, but their cultural differences are often greater than their cultural similarities.

The elderly of minority groups not only share the financial restrictions, the health concerns, and the family disruptions of old age with all other groups, but they may have additional difficulties. For example, older persons of Mexican, Asian, Cuban, American Indian, and many other backgrounds often do not speak English well and may not read any English at all. As their memory for recent events becomes poorer, the little English they have acquired may be forgotten. Therefore, to fill out forms, to communicate with a harried welfare worker, or to simply ask how to get to the right person to get the answer to a question seems an insurmountable task.

Also, our country's values have been mostly heavily influenced by Central and Northern European immigrants, in interaction with the streams from Southern Europe. Our values and expectations may be unfamiliar to persons arriving from Asia or Latin America or to those entering urban communities from Indian reservations. In Japan and China, for example, the elderly parents of a son are cared for by the son's wife, but many American or Canadian daughters-in-law of Asian ancestry are very unhappy with this role.

At the same time, elderly minority-group members must find some way of coping with the new militancy found among their young. The young people's behavior may violate the elderly people's long-internalized values regarding proper procedures and proper role-behavior. The elderly may be accused of behaving like Uncle Tom or Tío Taco or Uncle Tomatsu when they are merely adhering to long-held values that are difficult to change. Thus, many of the ethnic elderly have led a doubly difficult life. First, they are victimized by overt or covert prejudice and discrimination or by their lack of language skills, vocational training, and opportunity. (Sometimes, as in the case of the laws discriminating against Asians or the customs discriminating against blacks and Latinos, the differential in opportunity has been both extreme and inflexible.) Second, they now find themselves under attack for not having been aggressive enough at an earlier age against these injustices or for not being able to alter their values sufficiently in their later years.

In the last year or two, I have observed an increasing appreciation of the plight of the elderly of diverse ethnic groups, both by members of their own group and by the general community. More younger people from minority groups are becoming personally and professionally concerned with their elderly. For example, a group of young Japanese Americans established a facility where their elderly could (and, in substantial numbers, did) congregate; militant young blacks have escorted elderly blacks for shopping and other purposes to prevent their being robbed. At the professional level, groups like the National Caucus on the Black Aged have been established, and conferences on black aging have been run since 1971. A general conference on minority aging was launched in 1973. A geriatric day-care center has been established in San Francisco for elderly Chinese, Filipinos, and Italians; one set up in New York City is visited primarily by elderly Orthodox Jews, blacks, and Puerto Ricans.

Chapter Five

Physical and Social Environments

We live in time, in space, and in society; therefore, each of us must function within a time structure, a physical structure, and a social structure. These facts cannot be altered, although the specific natures of the structures are susceptible to change. For the older person, all three structures seem to be contracting.

Functioning in space becomes more difficult as physical movement is inhibited by arthritis or other factors reducing psychomotor effectiveness; the same factors may make driving more of a problem, and public transportation is often too expensive or inadequate. Functioning in society also has its problems, which were discussed in part in the section on disengagement. Functioning in time can be the most troublesome of all. On the one hand, time is running out; on the other hand, time may pass slowly, for available activities and relationships perhaps are not so stimulating or challenging or enjoyable as they once were.

In considering environments for the elderly, we must explore those that have been devised in other cultures as well as those devised by various subcultural groups within the United States and Canada (discussed in the previous chapter). Sweden, for example, provides extensive health and personal care systems for its elderly; England has a well-developed system of national health insurance; the Netherlands provides small plots of land near urban areas for the elderly who wish to garden. What effects do these structural differences in social systems have on the elderly?

Along the same line, and perhaps more to the point, what happens to the elderly whose social role in their communities differs greatly from that of our elderly? In a few subsistence societies, the elderly are killed— or kill themselves—when they become too old to provide useful services. (You have undoubtedly heard of societies that leave the old to die in the cold or to starve in the desert—an action that indicates not cruelty but simple inability to maintain a viable society if the elderly drain its resources.) Elsewhere, the elderly maintain rigid control of property until their deaths; sometimes the property is then passed down to the eldest son or, sometimes, to the widow. In one African culture, dependency is considered virtuous; as a result, the elderly can anticipate extensive support from family members, who feel guilt and suffer ostracism if they fail to honor their dependency (Shelton, 1969).

The social values and attitudes of the elderly themselves obviously vary both as a function of the values of the society in which they live and as a function of being old. Gerontologists are only beginning to look at this matter. For example, do the differences in religious values between elderly black Americans and younger black Americans parallel the differences between the elderly and the young among white or Mexican or Filipino Americans? Would a longitudinal study of rural women, beginning when the women were 40 and keeping track of them until the women were in their seventies, find the same kinds of changing views on the significance of education that would be found among urban women of the same social class, ethnicity, and age? Do Catholic sisters face death differently from women who have been public-school teachers or physicians or Protestant missionaries all their adult lives?

These are the kinds of issues that psychological gerontologists can explore from a variety of methodological viewpoints. In exploring them, we can attempt to differentiate those changes that are related to the aging process from those changes that are related to the circumstances of a particular age cohort in society.

I will begin this chapter with a brief discussion of the event that makes time so important: one's death. I will then discuss the physical environment, housing, and transportation. A brief comment on religion is followed by a section on work and retirement. A few final pages on ways of intervening to improve the elderly's environments and the implications of such interventions close the chapter and the book.

Facing Death

Death can come at any age, but today, more than at any time in the history of the world, death is predicted by age. Awareness of death, including one's own death, does not occur suddenly in old age, although the full impact of the significance of death can be felt in a dramatic moment, and this moment may occur during the later years.

When a young person is getting ready to enter college, graduation seems endless years away. Although he may make a few plans for the years after he graduates, and although he fully recognizes that the time will come when he will no longer be in college, it is difficult for him to plan for this eventuality. As he enters his senior year, and with increasing frequency as the year slips by, he begins to think in terms of how many days, weeks, months, exams, term papers, or classes remain. He no longer speaks of having been in college for three and a half years but of how much time he still has left.

My metaphor must be obvious, except that the enormity and inevitability of dying place it in a category by itself. People often assume that death is more frightening for the elderly than for the young, perhaps because of its imminence. The evidence, however, indicates just the opposite. Although older people think about death more frequently, they are less afraid of it (Kalish & Reynolds, 1975). Older people seem to feel that they have lived their lives and have received what they felt they "had coming"; younger people contemplate their own death as coming too soon, as robbing them of their birthright. Many older people have been able to cope with their own eventual death partly because they have had to cope with a variety of other losses: the death of friends and family members, the loss of various functional abilities, youthful appearance, active roles, and important relationships.

During an interview, one 86-year-old man commented, "When you're as old as me . . . you'll learn that time devours you; it eats you right up." Toward the end of the same interview, he said "I'm doing nothing all the time, nothing. That's the worst punishment a man can have—nothing to do!" (Kastenbaum, 1966, p. 332). The dilemma of the elderly is that the weeks, months, and years zoom by at an accelerating pace, with only death at the end, while at the same time the minutes and hours can drag by when filled with nothing.

As time and their future become briefer, many elderly begin to reminisce, to review their lives. This life review can be extremely helpful in enabling the older person to see his life as an integrated whole rather than as a series of episodes, to reflect upon his accomplishments, and to deal with feelings of nostalgia and regret (Butler, 1963). Some older people begin to write their life histories, often at great length, with the dual motive of leaving something of themselves behind for their children and grandchildren and of seeing their entire past spread out before them.

The "trajectory" of dying is an expression proposed by two sociologists to describe the nature of the downhill path from normal health to death (Glaser & Strauss, 1968). For a cancer patient, the trajectory would move slowly and irregularly down; for a person suffering from a series of heart attacks, the trajectory would resemble a series of downward steps of different sizes; for a suicide, the trajectory would look like one large step. The way in which an individual dies is much more than the outcome of the way he lived. It also reflects his terminal condition, the kinds of care he receives, the degree to which he is sedated, the pain and discomfort he suffers, and the human relationships that surround him.

A well-known psychiatrist has suggested that five stages mark the normal and appropriate pathway to death, at least for those whose trajectories permit the time and the necessary awareness. These stages are (1) denial and isolation, (2) anger, (3) bargaining (attempts to postpone death), (4) depression, and (5) acceptance (Ross, 1969). Not every person goes through each stage in the sequence presented, and people may move back and forth between stages or may even be in two stages simultaneously. In the final stage, the dying person has come to accept impending death; he has made peace with himself and with others and is ready to die. In many ways, he is almost completely disengaged from everyone and everything except very close family members (perhaps only spouse and children, or even only spouse) and one or two friends and the hospital staff who, during his final days, are vitally important people to him (Ross, 1969). Although these stages have received considerable recognition, other writers have proposed other stages or have denied that any one sequence of stages is seen in more than a small proportion of the dying.

Many issues concerning death and dying are especially meaningful for the elderly. Whether a dying patient should be informed of his prognosis has been hotly debated, although most people say that they themselves would wish to know and admit that most dying people do know when they are dying, even if they are not directly informed (Kalish & Reynolds, 1975). Another important question is how long to use what the medical profession terms "heroic" methods to keep patients alive, especially when there is good evidence that extensive brain damage had already occurred. Closely related is the suggestion that people be permitted to dictate, while still healthy and alert, what should be done to them when they are in great pain or have suffered extensive brain damage—in other words, that they have the option to choose death through what is called a "living will."

Physicians, family members, and others, usually well meaning, may suggest to a terminally ill older person that he become resigned. "A counsel of resignation is not really counsel at all. It is a plea, if not a demand, that the aged person accept his foreshortened future and not ask his physician to intercede" (Weisman, 1972, p. 141). The elderly simply do not elicit the same reactions during their terminal stages that children do. "The terminally aged may be as helpless as a child, but they seldom arouse tenderness" (Weisman, 1972, p. 144).

Although it is very difficult for those who are not old to understand adequately what a dying elderly person must face, a noted psychiatrist has listed seven questions that each person can try to answer for himself in order to come a little closer to feeling what the elderly feel as they confront death:

1. If you faced death in the near future, what would matter most?
2. If you were very old, what would your most crucial problems be? How would you go about solving them?
3. If death were inevitable, what circumstances would make it acceptable?
4. If you were very old, how might you live most effectively and with least damage to your ideals and standards?
5. What can anyone do to prepare for his own death, or for that of someone very close?
6. What conditions and events might make you feel that you were better off dead? When would you take steps to die?
7. In old age, everyone must rely upon others. When this point arrives, what kind of people would you like to deal with [Weisman, 1972, p. 157]?

The Physical Environment

Until recently, behavioral scientists have ignored the influence on human behavior of the physical space within which the individual functions. Industrial studies have been made of the effects of lighting, color, and sound on behavior, but the general topic has received little attention. Conversely, those who design space—architects, planners, engineers, builders—have tended to ignore the characteristics of the people for whom they are designing, often emphasizing costs, efficiency of design, and their own esthetic preferences—all necessary factors for consideration, but not the whole story. Fortunately, those who design physical space and those concerned with human behavior are now sitting down and talking with each other.

Some kinds of physical space are used primarily to promote social interactions. Everyday experience tells us that discussion is carried on more easily when people face each other across a table, in a circle, or at right angles to each other. Nonetheless, seating in many institutional settings for the elderly is arranged so that the seats are all parallel to each other or all facing a television set. Often, in order to increase the amount of physical space in the center of a room, the seating is arranged along the walls, a design efficient in its utilization of space but inefficient for interaction. Healthy and socially aggressive younger persons might push the seats into better positions, but older people—especially those in institutions—often are too passive or lack the physical strength.

Since the design of buildings sets limits on the flexibility of interior physical space, planning for flexibility must begin early in the design process. In one high-rise apartment building for the well elderly, the mail is delivered to a centrally located counter, and the designers have created opportunities for social interaction by increasing the amount of surrounding space and placing chairs and tables and a supply of magazines at this place, where people normally congregate anyway. The result is a high degree of social interaction. Another plan for this building was to provide a small furnished space near the elevator where people could sit and talk, again making use of natural traffic patterns to encourage informal contacts. In another high-rise building, a small room set aside for reading and casual discussion failed in its purpose because people had to walk down a normally untraveled corridor to get there. Since the elderly residents had to plan ahead to go there, without knowing whether any companions would be in the room, the room was often empty.

Do older people prefer to be "where the action is" or to remain secluded and private? The obvious answer is that both options are important, and, if both are available to the elderly, their flexibility of functioning increases. In one housing project for the elderly, the main entrance opened on a lovely garden, surrounded by a wall and containing benches for sitting; the back of the building faced a moderately busy street. Although the garden benches were used, many of the elderly would take deck chairs to the back of the building, where they could view the street activity through the design of the stone fence, even though that space was cramped and not at all attractive.

The opportunity to alter physical space to suit individual needs and preferences is another necessity for the elderly. "To project one's personality upon a space, one must be able to change it" (Gelwicks, 1970, p. 155). Rooms in institutions for the elderly, and even the physical arrangements in a senior recreation center, are often designed so that the users can change them very little. The selection and arrangement of furniture, the decorations, and the color scheme are all established by professionals without involving the users in the decisions and without permitting subsequent change easily and inexpensively. Some institutions do not permit the elderly to bring in their own furniture or even to hang their pictures on the wall. Older people coming to an institution already feel that their power to influence their own lives has diminished greatly, and this inflexibility of room arrangements intensifies their sense of powerlessness and helplessness (Gelwicks, 1970).

Some special physical environmental necessities arise for the elderly whose health or strength is impaired. The most obvious ones are grip bars for the bathtub and shower, stoves that are designed so that the user does not have to lean across the burners to reach the oven or things above the oven, and doorways wide enough for the wheelchairs and without risers that might trip elderly occupants. Other needs are less obvious. Arthritic hands may require special knobs on kitchen and other types of equipment; visual limitations can obscure spatial boundaries (between wall and floor, between the edge of the top step and the space beyond it), and these boundaries can be marked with contrasting paint; strength limitations may make it difficult to get up from a soft-cushioned couch that lacks rigid armrests.

Many other environmental considerations are particularly relevant for the elderly:

> high curbstones
> high steps for mounting buses
> traffic lights of short duration, especially on wide streets that lack a median strip
> broken sidewalks or flagstone walkways
> too much glare
> too little light
> institutions in which all rooms have the same shape and the same furniture selection and location (confused older people can end up in the wrong room)

I have barely touched the surface of this topic. The following sections on housing and transportation will discuss it further.

Housing

Of all heads of household over 65 years of age, 70% own their own homes (Brotman, 1972). This statistic may surprise you, but, since many older persons are not heads of household, the figure does not imply that 70% of all older persons live in a home they own. Neither should this figure be interpreted to mean that older people have no housing problems. First, a high proportion of their homes are extremely old and often run-down; second, many are located in high-crime areas, where older people are especially likely to be victims; third, rising property taxes often take a substantial portion of the older person's income, leaving no money for repairs; and, finally, the elderly often remain in these homes because they have no adequate alternative.

One apparent solution for the older homeowner is to sell his home and then rent slightly smaller facilities with the money obtained. In practice, this solution is frequently impossible. The average value of the home owned by a person over 65 is under $15,000 (Brotman, 1972). Selling costs and capital-gains taxes would consume a portion of this amount, and moving expenses would take an additional portion. Even assuming, however, that the individual could net $15,000 through such a sale, by investing that amount in the bank at normal interest rates, he could not obtain very much in the way of housing. If he wished to draw from the principal to add to the interest for rent payments, his capital would eventually run out and he would be in danger of having no money at all. This situation is typical of the financial conflicts that the lower-income elderly face.

In truth, most older people are satisfied with their present housing. They are especially unhappy about attempts to move them out of their neighborhoods (Lawton & Nahemow, 1972). These attempts were a great problem during the 1960s, when urban renewal forced so many elderly people, especially the low-income and nonwhite elderly, from their homes and neighborhoods.

Several varieties of housing are available for the elderly as alternatives to owning or renting their own home. Mobile homes are very popular among older people; over half of the residents at some trailer courts are retired. Many of the elderly find the low cost and informality of such facilities very attractive; others are put off by the lack of privacy and the limited amount of room in mobile homes. Another alternative is the retirement hotel, usually an old hotel or apartment house, often in the downtown area of a city. It may provide limited services, such as maid service or a common meal service in the dining room. Unlike mobile-home parks, which are normally located on the outskirts of a town, the retirement hotel is located in the middle of "the action," providing the elderly access to more activities but increasing their chances of being victimized by crime.

Other older people live with family members, particularly brothers and sisters and adult children. Although most elderly people are very reluctant to live with their children, limited finances, health problems, or physical disabilities sometimes force them into such arrangements. One-third of those over age 65 who have living children do live with their children; normally, these children are themselves old enough that their children (the elderly parents' grandchildren) no longer live at home (Troll, 1971).

During the past two decades, many elderly people have moved into retirement communities, primarily established in California, Arizona, and Florida. Some of these villages restrict their residents to persons in or beyond their fifties (rules vary from village to village). Homes are purchased, normally on a very long-term payment plan, by individuals who have retired with a good income and are seeking a community offering a variety of activities for people of their own age group.

The pros and cons of living in these retirement communities have produced some very heated disagreements among gerontologists and among the elderly themselves. The controversies revolve around these communities' policies of age segregation, which restrict one's neighbors to other elderly people, and the communities' often semi-isolated location.

Although residents of retirement communities do admit to having less contact with family members than do elderly residents of the general community, they seem to have more friends available, have generally higher morale, and perceive their own health as better (Bultena & Wood, 1969). Although they miss the stimulation of mixing with younger people and children on a regular basis, older persons appear to have more social contacts and greater life satisfaction when they live in communities with high proportions of other older people (Rosow, 1967). Furthermore, extensive contact with younger adults and children is not an unmixed blessing. Not only do tensions arise regarding life-style, manners, and appropriate behavior, but the noise and sudden movements of young children are often disconcerting for the elderly.

Retirement communities are certainly not for all older persons. They are often isolated from activity centers, their houses are expensive to purchase, and the pressures they exert on people to participate in activity programs are often extreme (at least they have been in the past); but they do represent a significant option for living arrangements for the elderly who can afford them.

Institutional Care

Few matters pertaining to the elderly have caused greater unhappiness than institutional care. Not only have the facilities providing the care come under frequent attack for their inadequacies—both social and physical—but the economic cost of institutional care is immense, and Medicare payments often fall far short of covering the expense. As stated in Chapter One, although only 5% of the elderly are in an institution at any one time, an estimated 20 to 25% or more spend some time in such a facility.

When we think of an institution for the elderly, we are likely to have an image of a nursing home, sometimes called a convalescent-care facility. These institutions care for those elderly people who need considerable attention, either because of physical problems or because of mental confusion. Some nursing home residents are highly debilitated; they may sit and stare all day long at a television set without really knowing what they see; they can be incontinent, unable to feed themselves, or apparently unaware of where they are or even who they are. Some health-care professionals describe feeding them with the grotesque expression (perhaps used in an attempt to cope with their own discomfort) "time to water the vegetables."

Although very few elderly people ever reach this stage, and although the condition of some who seem to have declined to that stage could be improved through proper psychosocial treatment, many laymen conjure up exactly this image when they think of "the old folks." This misperception is not limited to the nonelderly. Often an 80-year-old will be heard referring to "the old people," meaning people in nursing homes. Such an image of aging and of institutions has been one of the factors causing people to wish to have as little contact as possible with the elderly.

Another geriatric institution is the home for the aged, or the board-and-care home. These are geared for people who require some help or supervision but who can basically care for themselves. The residents can often bathe and feed themselves and are unlikely to be very confused. These facilities emphasize social services rather than health-care services. Social interactions are more frequent, and activity programs are often planned.

A third category, established more recently, is that of the intermediate-care facility, which tries to fill the gap often left between the nursing home and the home for the aged.

In practice, however, divisions among these three levels of care are not so clear as they are in theory. An elderly person may end up in a particular home—one that may be inappropriate for him—because it is run by the church, because a physician had heard it gave better care than the more appropriate facility, because of expense, or because no appropriate facility is located nearby.

Relatively few long-term care facilities have attempted to provide intellectual or sensory stimulation for their patients. This lack is particularly true of nursing homes, in part because the cost of running a nursing home is so high that additional staff is taken on only with great reluctance, and in part because the responsiveness of many of the patients is so minimal that only the most persevering worker will continue to try to elicit their reactions. Unfortunately, the more the staff members fail to interact with the patients, the more they do things for the patients instead of taking the extra time to help the patients do things for themselves, the more—in short —they give up on the patients, the more the patients sink into despondency and turn their thoughts and feelings inward.

Most nursing home staff members have had no training in the field before coming to the home, receive little or no in-service training, and are very poorly paid. Relatively few of them enjoy the tasks they are required to perform, and many are not particularly attracted to working with people as confused and sick as nursing home patients often are.

Administrators are frequently so involved with the immediate and highly demanding problems of day-to-day functioning that they have little time to consider staff training and little energy to encourage the necessary programs and social interactions that might help their patients. Lacking cognitive or sensory stimulation, those patients who are already ill and confused become more so. Yet to place full blame on the owners and administrators is to overlook the fact that minimal amounts of money are provided for nursing home care, even with the support of Medicare and Medicaid, and the fact that maximum demands are made on the time and energy of administrators. (One administrator referred to himself and his colleagues as the "human garbage collectors," not because he felt that way about his patients but because he felt that society in general regarded him in that fashion.)

Making matters worse is the sad fact that a life must end in the depersonalized atmosphere of an institution, away from the friends and family and community among whom that life was lived. The truth is well known both to the elderly who enter these institutions and to all others: for most, it is a final stopping place before their death. One retired economics professor, who entered a nursing home shortly before his ninety-third birthday, wrote:

> There are very few of the kind of people that I'd like to associate with here in the hospital. The men are old and decrepit. The women are similar. Only one or two that are out of the ordinary in looks. I miss my neighbors of the past. But since it cannot be helped I must put up with it. The food and service are excellent. My son and wife are about four minutes away from me. This is not an ordinary hospital. People come and stay until they die. I undoubtedly am in that class.

Another institution for the elderly is the state psychiatric hospital, although the recent trend has been for these hospitals to return their patients to the community or, often, to send them to long-term care facilities, which are—in turn—often loath to accept any mental patients whose symptoms might upset the other patients or be especially troublesome to the staff.

Although institutional care often reduces the individual's potential for mastery of his environment and development of his strengths, it may provide the best available alternative among those open to him. In evaluating the appropriateness of institutionalization, not only the elderly person himself but others in his family need to be considered. In some instances, when proper programs are available, institutional treatment can change behavior in a positive fashion; but nursing homes unfortunately do not often have social-therapeutic programs and are not reimbursed by Medicare or Medicaid when they do put such programs into effect (Gottesman, Quarterman, & Cohn, 1973).

> In sum, with advancing age an increasingly high proportion of old persons reaches institutions. When found in the institutions, over 30% are bedridden, about 25% are incontinent, and the majority are constantly disoriented for time, place, and persons, have gross memory defects, obvious difficulties in doing the simplest of calculations, as well as a dearth of general information . . . The patient's needs are such that it can be said:

"If medical care is good, psychiatric care should be improved; if both are good, social services should be improved; if all are good, all should be improved" [Goldfarb, 1969, pp. 303–304].

Relocation

Americans are a highly mobile population, moving from house to house and from community to community in great numbers. Older people are also mobile; considerable movement occurs among them at the time of retirement, when some leave their homes and relocate in the "sunshine states." Others move closer to their children, leave farms and move to nearby towns, or leave home communities for retirement villages. All moves, no matter how unpleasant the house being vacated and how pleasant the new accommodations, introduce at least minimal stress. Not only do new social relationships replace familiar ones, but new kinds of physical space must be dealt with: shopping, visits to physicians, local transportation facilities, and movie theaters and other sources of entertainment.

Assuming that older people carefully consider the pros and cons of relocation, such moves can be to their advantage. One healthy 80-year-old man and his 70-year-old wife left Cleveland, Ohio, where they had lived all their lives, for a Florida condominium. In Florida, they could walk out their front door 52 weeks each year and were virtually assured of finding someone they knew; many other local residents were longtime friends, and many Cleveland friends came to Florida to visit. In Cleveland, the weather and the structure of buildings worked against casual and spontaneous social contacts, but the Florida arrangement encouraged them. (Incidentally, the couple spent two winters renting in this development before they decided to relocate.) Obviously, only a minute percentage of older people can afford such a move. For the most part, older people are less mobile than younger people for economic, health, and psychological reasons.

Relocation of an entirely different type has become a major concern: moving the elderly person into a convalescent-care facility or from one institution to another. During the first year after admission, the death rate among the elderly in nursing homes is substantially higher than actuarial expectations for those of their age group and higher than the death rate of those of their age group on the waiting list (Lieberman, 1961). Part of this difference could be attributed to the more serious health condition of those entering, but this factor does not completely account for it. People transferred from one convalescent-care facility to another also show a substantial increase in incidence of death, although the relocation effects are apparently restricted to those suffering serious mental or physical impairment prior to the transfer (Goldfarb, Shahinian, & Burr, 1972).

Understanding the causes for this increased death rate is difficult, but it appears logical that elderly people who are already slightly confused or who have some difficulty mastering their physical environment will find adjusting to change a very troublesome matter. Not only is the change psychologically distressing, but they are likely to find old habits difficult to break. For example, even the most alert person tends to be slightly disoriented while getting up to go to the toilet in the middle of the night (a necessity more common among the elderly than among younger persons anyway). When an unexpected doorway or chair gets in the way, an elderly person is more likely to lose his balance and, if he does fall, is more likely to break a bone. Moreover, in strange surroundings, an older person is more likely to wander into the wrong room, take a short walk outside the institution grounds and get lost, or do something else that brings him to the attention of the institution's administrators. Increased restrictions may then be placed upon his freedom, causing even greater feelings of helplessness.

Essentially, the reaction termed *relocation shock* may well result from an interaction between the difficulties in moving through the new physical environment and the confusion and distress caused by having to deal with the unfamiliar.

Transportation

People need to move through physical space as well as reside within it, and transportation is one of the greatest needs of the elderly in the United States and Canada. Relatively few cities have adequate public-transportation systems, and, even when the transportation is adequate, its design may make utilization troublesome for the elderly. Even more important, the life pattern in most sections of America presupposes that virtually everyone has an automobile available. Yet nearly 45% of households headed by a person 65 or over have no car, a figure three times as high as the figure for persons between 26 and 64 (Revis, 1971). Limited income and physical disabilities combine to produce this low percentage of car owners among the elderly.

Although many elderly people walk a great deal, others tire quickly or have medical conditions that preclude extensive walking. Moreover, many services and activities are located too far from older people's homes to permit walking. Thus, without cars, unable to walk long distances, and lacking adequate and low-cost transportation, older people frequently find themselves physically cut off from important people and necessary services.

Some action has been taken to ameliorate these conditions. Many communities have arranged for reduced fares on public transportation,

Table 5.1. Percentage of older people visiting specified destinations by time required to reach destination (in minutes for one-way trip) and by frequency of trip. Based on 709 retired older persons, San Antonio, Texas, interviewed in 1968 and 1969. (Number of persons varies with destination.) (Carp, undated.)

Destination	Time in Minutes			Frequency					
	Less than 15	15 to 30	30 or More	Daily	2 or 3 per Week	Weekly	1 to 3 per Month	1 to Several per Year	Every 2 or 3 Years or Never
Friends	61%	33%	6%	12%	11%	12%	16%	10%	40%
Children	37	33	30	6	7	12	11	16	47
Other Kin	35	29	36	4	5	10	14	18	49
Doctor	45	42	13	0	1	4	23	54	19
Church	75	24	1	2	7	39	10	7	34
Grocery	77	20	3	5	28	36	13	<1	18
Other Stores	54	41	5	1	3	11	30	32	23
Meetings	58	37	5	<1	3	4	18	2	71
Entertainment	58	40	2	0	1	2	7	10	79
Senior Center	84	15	1	<1	2	2	2	2	91
Library	69	28	3	1	2	2	4	3	87
Sports	23	51	27	0	1	2	1	6	90

although often these fares are limited to off-hours. Occasionally an agency arranges for special vehicles to pick up older people for shopping, doctor visits, nutrition or recreation programs, or pleasure trips. If a general shift to public transportation occurs as a result of the recent realization that automobile traffic contributes disproportionately to environmental hazards, the elderly will probably benefit. Some recent experiments in substantially reducing the fares of such transportation will also encourage use by older people.

Religion and the Aging

Are older people more religious than younger people? Do people become more religious as they grow older? These two questions, interrelated but not identical, have received some preliminary answers, but final conclusions still cannot be drawn. One major impediment to conclusive answers is that the definition of "religious" is so open to debate. For example, research results are quite different if we define "religious" in terms of church attendance as opposed to belief in God.

One source distinguishes five dimensions of religiousness: religious practices, religious beliefs, religious knowledge, religious experiences, and consequences of religion on personal and social life (Glock & Stark, 1965). Rather than assume any single dimension or any combination of dimensions to be the definition of "religiousness," this approach looks at each dimension separately. For example, church attendance rises with age until the later years and then gradually declines, probably due to difficulties in transportation, health, and income. Similarly, although church membership among older persons is more common than all other social-organization memberships combined, active church involvement diminishes slightly in the later years. On the other hand, listening to church services on the radio and television, praying, Bible reading, and meditating all increase steadily with age (Moberg, 1971).

If we look at all of these measures, it appears that religious practice is greater among older persons and would be greater still were it not for the limitations of income, health, and mobility. How many of these age differences result from changes that occur with age and how many arise from differences in upbringing between persons born at the turn of the century and those born later is still unknown. Perhaps both factors contribute.

The elderly also retain more traditional religious beliefs than younger persons do. For example, belief in God and in immortality has been shown to be greater among the elderly (Moberg, 1971). Studies of religious knowledge, however, provided less consistent results; the elderly are apparently better versed in certain religious matters and younger persons are more informed on others. Since the elderly have less formal education and may also be troubled by slower reaction time (if the test is timed) or lack of test sophistication, religious knowledge is difficult to evaluate.

"Many older people experience religious feelings, emotions, thoughts, visions, and dreams and share them with clergymen, relatives, and friends, even though they do not often talk with their physicians about them" (Moberg, 1971, p. 29). Again, concrete evidence is lacking, but clinicians' impressions suggest an increase in these experiences with age.

The impact of the final dimension distinguished by Glock and Stark, consequences of religion on personal and social life, is almost impossible to judge because of the difficulty in deciding what the consequences should be. For example, if you believe that the consequences should include a willingness to become a missionary serving one's religion, you will arrive at a conclusion on the impact of religion and its relationship to age considerably at variance with the conclusion drawn by the person who believes that the consequence should be a diminution of ethnic prejudice and discrimination.

The relevance of religion and the church to the elderly goes beyond the belief systems of individual older people. Many churches have space that is unused during the workweek—perhaps the only such space in the community—and this space can be used to provide senior recreation, hot meals, or continuing-education programs. Furthermore, hospital chaplains are in a particularly good position to discuss with elderly patients their concerns about their illness, their eventual death, and, of course, their families, activities, and ongoing lives. Whereas physicians and nurses are perceived by patients as having other things to do, the chaplain is seen specifically as serving the spiritual and emotional needs of the patients.

Finally, the community clergyman and the pastoral counselor both offer valuable counseling services to the elderly. Many older persons lack both the money and the desire to ask for help from professional psychotherapists, but they will feel free to call upon their minister or priest or rabbi for help or to visit a pastoral counselor. In some instances, these clerical figures know the entire family of the elderly person, and they may be in a better position to provide counsel than anyone else.

Work and Retirement

The transition from work to retirement is one of the major changes occurring in the later years. Although in the past retirement has been primarily a concern for men, increasing numbers of women have entered the labor force during the past decade, abetted by pressures from the women's movement. Work—and therefore retirement—will be a vital consideration for women as well in the future.

It is easy to become trapped in the present, to assume that what exists today has always existed. Retirement is a new institution. Up until a few decades ago, the rich could retire, but other people had to work until poor health, physical handicaps, or inability to find a job forced them out of the job market. In 1900, 68% of American men 65 years of age and older were working, whereas, by 1960, the proportion had been halved to 32%; a further drop to 23% is anticipated by 1975 (Riley et al., 1968). Among older women, the percentage who are working has remained roughly the same over the 60-year period, although the proportion of all adult women working has gone up substantially.

Expectations of retirement and the actualities of retirement often turn out to be quite different. Furthermore, when middle-aged people—adult children, personnel directors, social workers, or gerontologists—try to project themselves into their own retirement years, their projections do not always help them understand people who are presently retired. People with young children, with rising status and power, with increasing income and increasing consumption patterns, and without aches and pains on arising in the morning are likely to lack a real awareness of what retirement offers, both positively and negatively, for the retired person.

Many work organizations have established an arbitrary mandatory retirement age, often 65, for most positions, although it may range as high as 70 and some individuals can be kept on on a year-to-year basis if they are shown to be nonexpendable. Such arbitrary limits on work life have been attacked by many elderly people and their supporters as violating a person's right to work. The rules are supported, on the other hand, by a combination of union policies, management preferences, and a growing influx of younger workers.

In previous eras, more people were self-employed and therefore could establish their own retirement age—in those rare instances in which they could afford not to work. More alternatives were available: an older person could switch to part-time work and turn over some responsibility for the farm or shop to a relative or a younger associate; he was able to slow his work pace or change to less demanding work. But these options are normally not open to the factory worker, civil-service employee, schoolteacher, or executive; all must abide by organizational regulations.

Nonetheless, only 21% of the wage-earning and salaried workers retiring in 1963 did so because of mandatory-retirement policies. True, this percentage was almost double the 11% of 1951 (Palmore, 1964), but there is little reason to believe that the trend toward mandatory retirement has increased much since 1963. These relatively low figures do not make retirement life any easier for those forced to retire against their will, but they at least suggest that the effects of arbitrary mandatory retirement age may not be so great as is often believed.

Nonetheless, in spite of the many discussions of the importance of feeling meaningful, of having job-related status, and of liking the social relationships that work provides, the one thing that retirees report that they miss most (and that those still employed anticipate missing most when they retire) is still *money!* In one study, nearly half of those retired cited money as the most serious retirement-related loss (Shanas, Townsend, Wedderburn, Friis, Milnoj, & Stehouwer, 1968b).

Physical and Mental Health

The folklore of aging has it that retirement causes major emotional problems and frequently leads to increased physical-health problems. Everyone has at least one tale to tell about a friend or acquaintance who was in excellent health until he retired, but then quickly became morose and depressed, then physically ill, and soon died (or at least died psychologically).

The evidence suggests just the opposite, quite consistently and quite emphatically. A review of the research on the health of recent retirees found many more reports of improved health than of health decrements (Eisdorfer, 1972). Since some jobs require work that is physically or intellectually strenuous, some reports of improved health after retirement undoubtedly merely reflect the opportunity to leave the rigorous demands and stresses behind.

Retirement trends between 1951 and 1963 show an increase in the proportion of persons who made the decision for retirement on their own (from 54% in 1951 to 61% in 1963) and a comparable decrease for those whose retirement was required by their employers. Although poor health accounted for one-third of the retirement decisions (down from 40% in 1951), one-sixth of those who retired in 1963 did so to enjoy leisure (nearly six times the proportion doing so in 1951). These data apply only to wage-earning and salaried workers, however, and do not include either professional, self-employed, or upper-echelon managerial persons or low-income, part-time, or seasonal workers who are paid by the hour (Palmore, 1964).

Finances

The economic aspects of retirement loom large both for the employing organization and for the person about to retire. From the organization's point of view, older workers are likely to be at the top salary for their level, and their benefits may cost more. From the worker's point of view, Social Security and other retirement plans provide at least a minimum amount of income, and some retirees can add income from other sources and attain a moderate, or even good, standard of living. Expenses in retirement may diminish somewhat, although probably less than most people anticipate.

Interpersonal Relationships

In the past, social relationships on the job have been considered one of the most important factors in job satisfaction and, for the same reasons, one of the major losses suffered in retiring. Although this is undoubtedly still the case in many communities and in many work organizations, in North American society as a whole, work associations may be losing some of their outside-of-work influence. Nonetheless, one-sixth of the respondents in one study reported that their greatest loss in leaving work was contact with their friends (Shanas et al., 1968b).

As retirement approaches, the worker finds that other employees are beginning to plan for his successor and to function as though he were already absent; in other words, those in his work milieu have begun to disengage. If he has an administrative or supervisory position, others are already vying for his job; if he is a teacher, the principal no longer appoints him to committees, and other teachers no longer include him in their plans for future programs.

Returning to visit the business or factory or organization after retirement can also be disappointing. After the first visit, which often meets with an enthusiastic reception, the visitor finds that other employees have new topics of conversation, new subjects for gossip, new work roles and staff alliances. They have advanced the process of disengagement quite effectively, and they often are uncomfortable when the retiree does not disengage also.

The Work Itself

Relatively few people really enjoy the tasks they are required to perform on their jobs, although they do like many of the relationships, the feeling of usefulness, and the money that come with work. Given the option of having time free from onerous tasks they have been performing for 45 years, they accept, but not without concern over what they have lost. In the study by Shanas and her associates (1968b), less than one-fifth of the retirees reported missing the work itself.

Although upper-echelon employees, managers, and professionals seem to have the greatest involvement in their work, there is little evidence whether they perceive their loss through retirement as greater than do other groups. Part of the difficulty in gathering conclusive evidence is that these people also have the highest retirement incomes and tend to have ongoing interests outside their previous jobs. Again we are confronted with the question of how much one's previous life history affects his ability to deal with an age-related change: are those best able to adjust to retirement the people who have lost or changed their status the least, or those who have had the most successful and satisfying work lives to look back on?

Ability and Power

Many kinds of job-related skills require constant updating, an effort that can become increasingly frustrating in the later years. Younger workers may already be trained in the newer skills, whereas older workers may need retraining at some expense to their organization. Unfortunately for the older worker, learning these new skills is not made easier—and is often made more difficult—by lengthy experience with previous skills. Individuals opting for early retirement were shown by one study to be beset by problems in meeting work demands and by inability to control the speed and pace of their work (Barfield & Morgan, 1969).

Although the ability to perform certain specific tasks may diminish with age, competence in many jobs does not diminish at all and may actually be greater at the time of retirement. Whether the individual's work capability actually is reduced or is merely believed by the organization to be reduced, the impact is still the same: he retires at the indicated age. And imminent retirement also causes a reduction in the employee's power and influence. Not only does he lack the power to retain his position—even top management personnel are often without the power to keep themselves entrenched beyond the mandatory retirement age—but his limited job future permits others to bypass him in many ways. Conversely, since the employee who is about to retire may have begun to disengage from his organization and to adapt to aspects of his coming role as retiree, he may no longer exercise the power he still retains.

Meaningfulness

For some people, work provides the major source of meaning in their lives. Without the opportunity to work, life appears hollow and without challenge. When asked what he would bring to a desert island if he were stranded with a dozen others for the rest of his life, one research-oriented professor responded "my typewriter, lots of paper, and books." Meaningfulness of work inheres in some people because they thoroughly enjoy their jobs: given the chance to do anything they wished, they would choose to do pretty much what they are doing. For others, the meaning of work has a more religious overtone: for them, work is a given "good" and a way of fulfilling their mission on earth.

In spite of the thorough enjoyment of work for some and the mystical quality of work for others, only 8% of Shanas' sample of retired persons stipulated the loss of work itself as the most important in retirement, although—interestingly enough—19% of those interviewed who were still employed believed that this loss would be paramount (Shanas et al., 1968b).

Perhaps those in actual retirement felt less concerned about the meaningfulness of work because they had found other satisfying tasks. Or perhaps they felt that they had justified their existence through many years of work and were now entitled to relax and enjoy their leisure. Whatever the process, concern over loss of the meaningfulness that work affords may be much more valid for those who saw their jobs as giving their lives more meaning and power.

Early Retirement

Hundreds of thousands of workers in the United States and Canada have been retired from one position, complete with benefits, by their mid-fifties and sometimes as early as their late thirties. Except for a handful of the very wealthy, these early retirees are primarily military men, firemen, policemen, and other civil servants. Most go on to take another job.

Another group is beginning to retire early, although under different conditions: those with adequate pensions who prefer freedom from the restrictions of work to its benefits. These people may retire only a few years before they reach the normal retirement age for their company, but they do it because they want to. In 1966, one-third of the respondents in a national sample indicated that they planned to retire before age 65 (Barfield & Morgan, 1969).

One study of auto workers who were given the option of early retirement is illustrative. Satisfaction with retirement, both for those who retired early and for those who waited until the regular retirement age, was greater when (1) the retirement was planned, (2) the retiree's health was good, (3) his standard of living was as good or better than before retirement, (4) his income had been relatively high, (5) his education was more extensive, and (6) the company he worked for has a preretirement program (Barfield & Morgan, 1969).

When the early retirees were compared with those who chose to remain on the job, a number of differences were found, none of them especially surprising. Early retirees were in a better financial position. They also had spent more time discussing retirement with others. Some job-related factors were also important: early retirees were more likely to have experienced recent change in the nature of their jobs, to feel that commuting was an irritation, or to find it difficult to keep up with their work demands or to control the pace of their work (Barfield & Morgan, 1969).

These data again show that, to understand a phenomenon such as retirement, we need to examine the characteristics of both the individual and the situation in which he finds himself—and, of course, the characteristics of the interaction between the two.

Life-Styles in Retirement

Life-styles in retirement certainly reflect earlier life-styles, although conclusions on the exact relationships are hard to draw. Most of those who are old today have not perceived many (if any) alternative life-styles. They worked hard—or at least felt they should—in order to achieve certain goals, and they have often carried this orientation into retirement. Younger people have chosen among a greater range of alternatives, including the choice of rejecting the entire premise that work is necessary for personal fulfillment or income. How these young people will eventually deal with retirement would make a fascinating longitudinal study. Lowenthal (1972) discusses this issue and then outlines nine life-styles that influence retirement, five of which she discusses in some detail.

1. The obsessively instrumental style. People following this life-style are seen by a casual observer as highly engaged. They appear to be task-oriented, driven to be involved, and, even in their leisure, compulsively active.

2. The instrumental/other-directed style. For these people, work provides access to satisfaction gained from others, particularly in meeting dependency needs. When these people retire, they will have to devise some alternative sources of satisfaction.

3. The receptive/nurturant style. Such individuals have developed "networks of close personal relationships" (Lowenthal, 1972, p. 321). Although this style is commonly associated with the traditional female role, men are also able to follow it. Retirement seems to have little effect on these people, except to require them to develop social networks outside the work situation. Retirement may be more destructive for those for whom work provided the greatest source of interpersonal satisfaction—such as teachers, social workers, or psychotherapists.

4. The autonomous style. Autonomous people are often creative and are necessarily able to initiate action and establish relationships as needed. The implication of the term "autonomous" is that these people are still enjoying personal growth. Loss of work roles should cause less interference in their lives than in the lives of other groups, because they can generate new roles and capacities.

5. The self-protective style. These people protect themselves from expressing their dependency needs, and they may well have established little engagement with life over the years. Therefore, retirement and concurrent disengagement are desired goals for them.

This list does not cover all the possible types of life-styles in retirement; indeed, there may well be better methods of establishing categories. Nonetheless, the five types are suggestive and can be used as a foundation for a well-considered study (Lowenthal, 1972).

Leisure Time in Retirement

Like many terms that defy precise and all-encompassing definition, "work" and "leisure" can be approached in various ways. One possibility is to differentiate leisure and work activities by whether or not they are income producing; another consideration is whether or not the activity is sought for pleasure. In the final analysis, we need to recognize that the concepts are blurred around the edges. For example, since I dislike gardening, gardening is work for me, whereas it is pleasure for many people; indeed, many older persons find gardening very relaxing and seek the opportunity to garden many hours each week. What about the person who gardens for other people for a living? Is that work? Is it work even if he thoroughly enjoys gardening and would rather garden than do anything else?

The kinds of leisure available are numerous, depending on the income, health, mobility, and personal preferences of the individual. Some of the most popular leisure activities of the elderly are gardening, reading, watching television, watching sporting events, participating in social activities, visiting friends and relatives, taking walks, and pursuing creative and educational interests.

The low-income elderly man in the inner city may spend much of his time sitting on a park bench and talking with friends or visiting a neighborhood senior center. His life may appear lonely to others, and, indeed, he may very well feel lonely and isolated; on the other hand, he may have developed the role of "loner" many years earlier and may actually prefer this kind of life pattern. A middle-income elderly couple still living in their suburban home may be socially active with friends, participate in political action, do volunteer work in a local hospital, or take up painting or ceramics. Again, their lives may appear full and rich to the outside observer, although many such persons report that they feel lonely, especially if their spouse has died. To understand the feelings of the older person, we need to know the actual nature of what he is doing, his previous life pattern, and his expectations and subjective perceptions.

While working—including doing housework and caring for children and others—an individual's time is structured by the demands of the work. In retirement, the day, the week, and the year may be without external structure, so that the individual must structure his own time. This task can be very difficult, and time can slip away in meaningless fashion—a disconcerting phenomenon for those who feel that time must be used profitably (however they define that term). Others take pleasure in unstructured time, whiling it away in casual pursuits.

Geriactivists (those elderly people who work actively to improve the lot of older people) and others who believe that meaning and purpose arise only from productive activity espouse the idea that all older persons need to be involved, and many retirees agree. After all, present opportunities for leisure were not available to many of today's elderly when they were young, and they often adhere to the work ethic. Atchley (1972) has surveyed the relevant research, including some of his own, and has come to the following conclusions on involvement:

1. Although retirees do feel a loss of involvement, this loss is not related to optimism or autonomy.

2. Retirees do maintain strong work orientations, but these beliefs are not accompanied by anxiety, depression, dislike of retirement, or withdrawal from activity.

3. Retirement life-style differs as a function of social class: those who had higher-status jobs are more work oriented, those who had middle-status jobs are more able to carry over their work-related tasks into retirement, and those who had lower-status jobs tend to engage in activities more oriented to things than to people or ideas.

4. The orientation of the retiree's former work—orientation to symbols, people, or things—carries over to the kinds of activities he prefers in retirement.

5. As time goes on, the opportunity for leisure during retirement will be more often seen as the worker's due reward than as in conflict with a work ethic.

These conclusions suggest that, as new generations move into retirement, they will be more eager to embrace the opportunity for leisure, assuming that their income and health are adequate. My personal belief is that those working with the elderly are overly concerned about retired people's inability to enjoy leisure because of the work ethic and insufficiently concerned with providing adequate options for the enjoyment of leisure. However, geriatricians are themselves work oriented and involved with symbols, and perhaps they project their own views and feelings onto the elderly with whom they work. It seems entirely possible that, given sufficient income and transportation, the elderly who are in good health would willingly make use of whatever sources of leisure entertainment were available without longing for work.

The working potential of the elderly has brought forth some penetrating controversies—controversies that are moral issues as much as social concerns. For example, in a period of fairly high unemployment, particularly among unskilled younger and minority workers, how much effort should be expended to keep the older worker on the job? Does this effort serve to undermine the unions' bargaining power? Are we encouraging work for the elderly because we don't wish to provide them with adequate income through Social Security? Should there be a "right to work" for the elderly that remains in effect after age 65? To some extent, the information discussed above is relevant to these issues, but each person will bring his own value system to bear in answering these questions.

Interventions with the Elderly

In the contemporary jargon, an "intervention" refers to an action planned by one individual or group to alter the life of another individual or group in a meaningful fashion, presumably for the better. Interventions with the elderly range from the establishment of senior centers to referrals for psychotherapy. We may also intervene by attempting to influence the elderly person's family members or to change the political system or the health-care system.

There are hazards involved in intervening in the lives of others. Sometimes the interveners are not so sensitive to the needs of those they want to help as they believe; sometimes people resent having others tamper with their lives, regardless of good intentions or even good outcomes; sometimes the cost of a planned intervention in money, time, and energy is much greater than it would have been if matters had been permitted to take their normal course.

Often, even the best of planned interventions have negative side effects. Returning nursing home patients to the community may improve the human relationships of some of the elderly, but this improvement can come at considerable cost in money and tension for those with whom they are now living. One intriguing study is worth special consideration. One group of elderly people living in the community were provided with a great variety of personal and health services without cost, while a control group were given only those services they normally received. After a period of time, the former group were found to have a slightly higher proportion of deaths, perhaps because they were caught up in a net of services that eventually led to institutional care and consequent relocation shock (Blenkner et al., 1971). This study is highly controversial, and its accuracy has been questioned. However, there is little doubt that there are many persons living in the community who, if given appropriate social services, would end up in a convalescent-care facility. Are they better off on their own in the community, often eating improperly or living in unclean conditions, or would they be better off in institutions that provide them with proper diet and care? The answer hinges on the meaning of "better off"—a phrase that is not easily defined.

Some attempts have been made to evaluate the effectiveness of various kinds of psychotherapy with the elderly. Group therapy was attempted with 54 mentally ill geriatric patients; the investigator concluded that the outcome was successful in terms of improved interpersonal relationships, control of temper tantrums, and better ward-adjustment (Wolff, 1963). Whether the improvement noted in this project and commented on by others who have tried group methods is a direct result of the therapy is difficult to ascertain. Perhaps increased attention from staff members or the establishment of informal discussion groups would have the same effects.

Psychotherapists, even today, appear to adhere to Freud's assumption that the elderly are not good candidates for psychotherapy. Various reasons are given: the elderly are too rigid; they do not have long enough to live to merit treatment; time is better spent with the young; old people are too confused or resistant or poor or. . . . The general consensus among professionals is that psychotherapeutic intervention is simply not appropriate for the elderly.

Although older persons rarely receive individual psychotherapy, the professional literature provides numerous accounts of successful therapy with these individuals (Oberleder, 1966; Wolff, 1963). With these cases, the traditional focus upon digging back into childhood memories and feelings received less emphasis, whereas more effort was made to understand present feelings, relationships, and circumstances. Some psychotherapists have advocated a more flexible therapeutic arrangement for the elderly, in which the therapist can serve as friend and helper (for example, answer simple questions about income tax, recommend an optometrist, or locate a travel agent), and does not have to adhere to the usual structure of a regular therapy session for a designated length of time.

Planned interventions, to provide optimum effectiveness, require evaluation. Proper evaluation will determine whether the intervention is successful, with "success" defined in terms of the goals of those planning the intervention. (If they have set up improper goals, this fact may or may not become apparent in time.) Evaluation can also be used to inform the interveners of possible improvements and appropriate changes, and a well-planned and well-conducted evaluation can provide information for other individuals and agencies who wish to establish similar programs.

Planned interventions, in the long run, must be related to general social policy. Therefore, the question arises: what is social policy regarding the elderly? To respond, we need to look at more limited issues, such as social policy on the provision of housing for low-income groups, social policy on convalescent-care facilities or geriatric day-care centers, or social policy on the financial responsibility of adult children toward their dependent parents. Also, social policy cannot always be determined on a nationwide basis; it often varies from region to region and sometimes varies from one community to an adjacent community. Social policy is not necessarily consistent, any more than the behavior of an individual is consistent; neither is social policy always enacted in actual programs, any more than your good intentions are always represented in your actual behavior and performance. It can be a useful exercise to try to learn about local social policies regarding the elderly on housing, transportation, recreation, mental and physical health, work, and so forth.

Many programmatic interventions involving the elderly are familiar to people working in the field. Some interventions are (1) senior centers that offer recreation, continuing-education programs, some health and (occasionally) legal services, and various kinds of information; (2) information and referral services that give relevant information in response to a telephone call or visit; (3) homemakers' services, including cooking and cleaning and providing social relationships—services that enable some elderly people to remain in their own homes rather than be relocated in institutions or other protective environments; (4) geriatric day-care facilities, in which older persons receive supervision and a variety of services during the day —usually restricted to individuals who are not capable of using senior centers; (5) nutritional programs, some of which transport recipients to a central location to eat and some of which, like the Meals-on-Wheels program, transport food to people who are not ambulatory; (6) the Foster Grandparent program, a federally subsidized program that pays low-income elderly people a small amount to care for, tutor, or play with institutionalized children; (7) the Retired Senior Volunteer Program, also federally subsidized, helping elderly persons to provide community services, but without recompense beyond reimbursement for local transportation and meals.

Other interventions on behalf of the elderly are the services of home-health aides (people who visit the nonambulatory elderly in their homes to provide health services); feeder bus systems (transportation systems that take people from their homes to regular bus, subway, or train stops); "sharing" groups (in which the elderly meet together, sometimes under professional supervision, to share their concerns and discuss possible solutions); nonprofit employment agencies established to help older people obtain employment; multiphasic health-screening programs, under which people can receive extensive diagnostic services at little or no cost; rent-supplement programs (providing the elderly with additional funds for housing so that they may obtain better housing in the community than they could otherwise afford); imposing credentials on nursing home administrators (requiring that they pass qualifying examinations); and political-action groups. Perhaps the interventions society has devised for the benefit of the elderly will never be sufficient, but they are a marked improvement over the virtual lack of such interventions 15 years ago.

Some Organizations Serving the Elderly in the United States

The *Administration on Aging* is part of the United States Department of Health, Education, and Welfare. It provides funds to carefully selected programs dedicated to improving the physical and personal conditions of the elderly. Among its recent concerns are improved nutrition, alternatives to institutionalization, and better housing and transportation. Although the AOA headquarters are in Washington, D.C., there are regional offices in major cities throughout the country. In addition, each state has a department on aging, funded partly through the AOA and usually located in the state capital.

The *American Association of Retired Persons,* in conjunction with the *National Retired Teachers Association,* is a private, nonprofit organization operated for the benefit of its membership, almost all of whom are elderly. It distributes a highly readable publication, offers health and automobile insurance, has its own travel agency, supplies low-cost pharmaceuticals by mail, and does some lobbying on behalf of the elderly. Dues are very low, and its membership numbers over 6 million.

The *American Geriatrics Society* restricts its membership to physicians with an interest in practice, administration, or research with the elderly.

The *Gerontological Society* has a membership consisting primarily of academics and other professionals concerned with the elderly and with the aging process. Most members participate in one of its four sections:

Biological Sciences, Clinical Medicine, Psychological and Social Sciences, and Social Research, Planning, and Practice. Some are members-at-large without sectional affiliation. Its headquarters are in Washington, D.C., but its annual meetings have been held in such cities as Miami, San Juan, Toronto, and Portland, Oregon.

The *Gray Panthers* are a political pressure group with a membership consisting primarily but not exclusively of older persons. As their name suggests, they are often militant in their demands, which include improved economic conditions and better health care.

The *National Caucus on the Black Aging* was initiated a few years ago in response to the feelings of many people that the black elderly could best be represented by other blacks. Its leadership consists of blacks, and its efforts are directed toward the problems of the black aging, but it simultaneously serves as advocate for elderly people in general, and it has many nonblack members. Its headquarters are in Washington, D.C.

The *National Council on Aging,* a volunteer agency headquartered in Washington, D. C., is a membership organization of professionals in the field of aging. Both individual and organizational memberships are available. The NCOA attempts to improve the condition and the image of all elderly people through providing information, holding national and regional meetings, planning and conducting educational and training programs, undertaking research, and publishing relevant materials. It is also involved in formulating public policy and in providing technical assistance to private and public agencies.

The *National Council of Senior Citizens* is primarily a membership organization of groups of retired people who are involved in advocating help for the elderly. They have a low-cost travel program, a low-cost drug-buying club, and low-cost insurance.

The *National Interfaith Coalition on Aging* attempts to disseminate information on aging and the elderly to church groups. The organization is very recently formed and is now conducting a major national study of resources, both present and potential, that exist for the elderly within various church denominations.

Senior Advocates has been recently instituted as a membership organization whose goals are to provide services for the elderly and to serve as their advocate in increasing available resources through both public and private sectors.

Other organizations include the Division of Adult Development and Aging, American Psychological Association; the Western Gerontological Society; the International Congress of Gerontology; the United States Senate Committee on Aging; and the National Institute of Aging, part of the National Institutes of Health.

Aging in the Future

What will the aging process be like in the future? What will it be like to be old in the future? Obviously, neither question can be answered with any certainty, but we can try out some hypotheses. For example, is it likely that life expectancy will be substantially greater 50 years from now? Or 100 years from now?

Some evidence exists that people in certain parts of the world have much higher life expectancies than people of the general middle-class American and Canadian community. An American physician who studied three communities, one in the Russian state of Georgia, one in the Andes, and one in Pakistan, concluded that "vigorous, active life involving physical activity (including sexual activity) was possible for at least 100 years and in some instances for even longer" (Leaf, 1973, p. 48). The communities he investigated followed practices, both physical and psychological, that are normally assumed to encourage good health. The entire matter, however, is still disputed.

It is possible that, in the future, we will know enough about the biochemistry of aging to intervene in the aging process directly, by altering body chemistry through some treatment, as well as indirectly, through improved diet and health care. We may attain this knowledge in the foreseeable future, perhaps within the next 30 to 50 years. Some research in slowing down the aging process in lower forms of animal life has been promising. This new knowledge would mean that, by the year 2000, extra years of healthy life (if the intervention does not add healthy years, it is of little value) may be added to life expectancy. If so, some social questions emerge: What will happen to mandatory retirement in the sixties? What population increases will ensue, and what impact will they have? What will result from the increase in five-generation families? What will be the political implications of a much larger population percentage over 65?

The next question, obviously, is whether society will be ready to deal with this change in life expectancy. We have not done an especially good job of enabling today's elderly to have a satisfying life; will we do better when the meaning of chronological age changes and more people live longer? Will the added years of vitality permit self-fulfilling activities and involvements and give people ample flexibility to select what they wish to do from a wide range of possibilities? Or will the added years signify a longer period in which to live with low income, limited resources, and low status? Many of you are likely to live long enough to learn the answers to these questions.

References

Aging, May 1970, **187,** 18–27.

Ahammer, I. M., & Baltes, P. B. Objective versus perceived age differences in personality: How do adolescents, adults and older people view themselves and each other? *Journal of Gerontology,* 1972, **27,** 46–51.

Atchley, R. C. *The social forces in later life: An introduction to social gerontology.* Belmont, California: Wadsworth, 1972.

Barfield, R., & Morgan, J. *Early retirement: The decision and the experience.* Ann Arbor, Michigan: Institute for Social Research, 1969.

Barrows, C. H., Jr. The challenge—mechanisms of biological aging. *The Gerontologist,* 1971, **11**(1, Pt. 1), 5–11.

Beckman, R. O., Williams, C. D., & Fisher, G. C. An index of adjustment to life in later maturity. *Geriatrics,* 1958, **13,** 662–667.

Bell, B., Wolf, E., & Bernholz, C. D. Depth perception as a function of age. *Aging and Human Development,* 1972, **3,** 77–82.

Bengtson, V. L. *The social psychology of aging.* Indianapolis: Bobbs-Merrill, 1973.

Bennett, R., & Eckman, J. Attitudes toward aging: A critical examination of recent literature and implications for future research. In C. Eisdorfer & M. P. Lawton (Eds.), *The psychology of adult development and aging.* Washington, D. C.: American Psychological Association, 1973.

Berardo, F. M. Survivorship and social isolation: The case of the aged widower. *The Family Coordinator,* 1970, **19,** 11–25.

Beresford, J. C., & Rivlin, A. M. *The multigeneration family. Occasional Papers in Gerontology,* Volume 3. Ann Arbor and Detroit: Institute of Gerontology, University of Michigan and Wayne State University, 1969.

Bergman, M. Changes in hearing with age. *The Gerontologist,* 1971, **11** (2, Pt. 1), 148–151.

Birren, J. E. *The psychology of aging.* Englewood Cliffs, New Jersey: Prentice-Hall, 1964.

Blenkner, M. Social work and family relationships in later life with some thoughts on filial maturity. In E. Shanas & G. F. Streib (Eds.), *Social structure and the family: Generational relations.* Englewood Cliffs, New Jersey: Prentice-Hall, 1965.

Blenkner, M. The normal dependencies of aging. In R. A. Kalish (Ed.), *Dependencies of old people.* In *Occasional Papers in Gerontology,* Volume 6. Ann Arbor and Detroit: Institute of Gerontology, University of Michigan and Wayne State University, 1969.

Blenkner, M., Bloom, M., & Nielsen, M. A research and demonstration project of protective services. *Social Casework,* 1971, **52,** 483–499.

Blum, J. E., Fosshage, J. L., & Jarvik, L. F. Intellectual changes and sex differences in octogenarians. *Developmental Psychology,* 1972, **7,** 178–187.

Botwinick, J. Geropsychology. In P. H. Mussen & M. R. Rosenzweig (Eds.), *Annual review of psychology.* Palo Alto, California: Annual Reviews, 1970. (a)

Botwinick, J. Learning in children and in older adults. In L. R. Goulet & P. B. Baltes (Eds.), *Life-span developmental psychology: Research and theory.* New York: Academic Press, 1970. (b)

Botwinick, J., & Thompson, L. W. Individual differences in reaction time in relation to age. *Journal of Genetic Psychology,* 1968, **112,** 73–75.

Britton, J. H., & Britton, J. O. *Personality changes in aging.* New York: Springer, 1972.

Bromley, D. B. *The psychology of human ageing.* Baltimore: Penguin, 1966.

Brotman, H. B. *Facts and figures on older Americans* (5, An Overview, 1971). Washington, D. C.: Department of Health, Education and Welfare, 1972.

Bühler, C. Old age and fulfillment of life with considerations of the use of time in old age. *Acta Psychologica,* 1961, **19,** 126–148.

Bultena, G. L., & Wood, V. The American retirement community: Bane or blessing? *Journal of Gerontology,* 1969, **24,** 209–217.

Busse, E. W. Theories of aging. In E. W. Busse & E. Pfeiffer (Eds.), *Behavior and adaptation in late life.* Boston: Little, Brown, 1969.

Butler, R. N. The life review: An interpretation of reminiscence in the aged. *Psychiatry: Journal for the Study of Interpersonal Processes,* 1963, **26,** 65–76.

Canestrari, R. E. Research in learning. *The Gerontologist,* 1967, **7**(2, Pt. 2), 61–66.

Carp, F. M. The mobility of retired people. *Transportation and aging: Selected issues.* Washington, D. C.: Government Printing Office, undated.

Case, H. W., Hulbert, S., & Beers, J. *Driving ability as affected by age* (Report 70–18). Institute of Transportation and Traffic Engineering, University of California at Los Angeles, 1970.

Cautela, J. A classical conditioning approach to the development and modification of behavior in the aged. *The Gerontologist,* 1969, **9,** 109–113.

Chen, Y. P. *Income* (White House Conference on Aging background papers). Washington, D. C.: Government Printing Office, 1971.

Chinn, A. B., Colby, E. S., & Robins, E. G. *Physical and mental health* (White House Conference on Aging background papers). Washington, D. C.: Government Printing Office, 1971.

Chown, S. M., & Heron, A. Psychological aspects of aging in man. In P. R. Farnsworth, O. McNemar, & Q. McNemar (Eds.), *Annual review of psychology,* **16,** 417–450. Palo Alto, California: Annual Reviews, 1965.

Cicchetti, D. V., Fletcher, C. R., Lerner, E., & Coleman, J. V. Effects of a social medicine course on the attitudes of medical students toward the elderly: A controlled study. *Journal of Gerontology,* 1973, **28,** 370–373.

Clark, M., & Anderson, B. G. *Culture and aging.* Springfield, Illinois: C. C. Thomas, 1967.

Cooper, R. M., Bilash, I., & Zubek, J. P. The effect of age on taste sensitivity. *Journal of Gerontology,* 1959, **14,** 56–58.

Corso, J. F. Sensory processes and age effects in normal adults. *Journal of Gerontology,* 1971, **26,** 90–105.

Cumming, E., & Henry, W. H. *Growing old.* New York: Basic Books, 1961.

Dennis, W. Creative productivity between the ages of 20 and 80 years. *Journal of Gerontology,* 1966, **21,** 1–8.

Eisdorfer, C. The WAIS performance of the aged: A retest evaluation. *Journal of Gerontology,* 1963, **18,** 169–172.

Eisdorfer, C. Intellectual and cognitive changes in the aged. In E. W. Busse & E. Pfeiffer (Eds.), *Behavior and adaptation in late life.* Boston: Little, Brown, 1969.

Eisdorfer, C. Developmental level and sensory impairment in the aged. *Journal of Projective Techniques and Personality Assessment,* 1960, **24,** 129–132. Reprinted in E. Palmore (Ed.), *Normal aging.* Durham, North Carolina: Duke University Press, 1970.

Eisdorfer, C. Adaptation to loss of work. In F. Carp (Ed.), *Retirement.* New York: Behavioral Publications, 1972.

Erikson, E. H. *Childhood and society.* (2nd ed.) New York: Norton, 1963.

Furry, C. A., & Baltes, P. B. The effect of age differences in ability: Extraneous performance variables in the assessment of intelligence in children, adults, and the elderly. *Journal of Gerontology,* 1973, **28,** 73–80.

Gelwicks, L. E. Home range and use of space by an aging population. In L. A. Pastalan & D. H. Carson (Eds.), *Spatial behavior of older people.* Ann Arbor and Detroit: Institute of Gerontology, University of Michigan and Wayne State University, 1970.

Glanville, E., Fisher, R., & Kaplan, A. Cumulative effects of age and smoking on taste sensitivity in males and females. *Journal of Gerontology,* 1965, **20,** 334–338.

Glaser, B. G., & Strauss, A. L. *Time for dying.* Chicago: Aldine, 1968.

Glock, C. Y., & Stark, R. *Religion and society in tension.* Chicago: Rand McNally, 1965.

Goldfarb, A. I. Masked depression in the old. *American Journal of Psychotherapy,* 1967, **21,** 791–796.

Goldfarb, A. I. Institutional care of the aged. In E. W. Busse & E. Pfeiffer (Eds.), *Behavior and adaptation in late life.* Boston: Little, Brown, 1969. (a)

Goldfarb, A. I. The psychodynamics of dependency and the search for aid. In R. A. Kalish (Ed.), *Dependencies of old people.* In *Occasional Papers in Gerontology,* Volume 6. Ann Arbor and Detroit: Institute of Gerontology, University of Michigan and Wayne State University, 1969. (b)

Goldfarb, A. I., Shahinian, S. P., & Burr, H. T. Death rate of relocated nursing home residents. In D. P. Kent, R. Kastenbaum, & S. Sherwood (Eds.), *Research planning and action for the elderly.* New York: Behavioral Publications, 1972.

Gottesman, L. E., Quarterman, C. E., & Cohn, G. M. Psychosocial treatment of the aged. In C. Eisdorfer & M. P. Lawton (Eds.), *The psychology of adult development and aging.* Washington, D. C.: American Psychological Association, 1973.

Gurin, G., Veroff, J., & Feld, S. *Americans view their mental health: A nationwide interview study.* New York: Basic Books, 1960.

Havighurst, R. J. Successful aging. *The Gerontologist,* 1961, **1,** 1–13.

Havighurst, R. J., & Albrecht, R. *Older people.* New York: Longmans, Green, 1953.

Havighurst, R. J., Neugarten, B. L., & Tobin, S. S. Disengagement and patterns of aging. In B. Neugarten (Ed.), *Middle age and aging.* Chicago: University of Chicago Press, 1968.

Hickey, T., Hickey, L., and Kalish, R. A. Children's perceptions of the elderly. *Journal of Genetic Psychology,* 1968, **112**, 227–235.

Hickey, T., and Kalish, R. A. Young people's perceptions of adults. *Journal of Gerontology,* 1968, **23**, 216–219.

Hill, R. Decision making and the family life cycle. In E. Shanas & G. Streib (Eds.), *Social structure and the family: Generational relations.* Englewood Cliffs, New Jersey: Prentice-Hall, 1965.

Howell, S. C., & Loeb, M. B. Nutrition and aging: Monograph for practitioners. *The Gerontologist,* 1969, **9**(3, Pt. 2), entire issue.

Hubert, A. Unpublished data, 1970.

Institute for Interdisciplinary Studies. *Older Americans speak to the nation—a summary* (White House Conference on Aging, background papers). Minneapolis, Minnesota, 1971.

Institute of Life Insurance. *Life insurance fact book.* New York, 1972.

Jackson, J. J. Sex and social class variations in black aged parent-child relationships. *Aging and Human Development,* 1971, **2**, 96–107.

Jarvik, L. F., & Blum, J. E. Cognitive declines as predictors of mortality in twin pairs: A twenty-year longitudinal study of aging. In E. Palmore & F. C. Jeffers (Eds.), *Prediction of life span.* Lexington, Massachusetts: Heath, 1971.

Jarvik, L. F., Kallman, F. J., & Falek, A. Intellectual changes in aged twins. *Journal of Gerontology,* 1962, **17**, 289–294.

Kahana, E., & Coe, R. M. Perceptions of grandparenthood by community and institutionalized aged. *Proceedings, 77th Annual Convention, American Psychological Association,* 1969, 735–736.

Kalish, R. A. The old and the new as generation gap allies. *The Gerontologist,* 1969, **9**(2, Pt. 1), 83–89. (a)

Kalish, R. A. Introduction. In R. A. Kalish (Ed.), *Dependencies of old people. Occasional Papers in Gerontology,* Volume 6. Ann Arbor and Detroit: Institute of Gerontology, University of Michigan and Wayne State University, 1969.

Kalish, R. A. Sex and marital role differences in anticipation of age-produced dependency. *Journal of Genetic Psychology,* 1971, **119**, 53–62.

Kalish, R. A. Of social values and the dying: A defense of disengagement. *The Family Coordinator,* 1972, **21**, 81–94.

Kalish, R. A., & Johnson, A. I. Value similarities and differences in three generations of women. *Journal of Marriage and the Family,* 1972, **34**, 49–54.

Kalish, R. A., & Reynolds, D. K. Death and bereavement in a cross-ethnic context. Unpublished manuscript, 1975.

Kaplan, H. B., & Pokorny, A. D. Aging and self-attitude: A conditional relationship. *Aging and Human Development,* 1970, **1**, 241–250.

Kastenbaum, R. As the clock runs out. *Mental Hygiene,* 1966, **50**, 332–336.

Kastenbaum, R., & Candy, S. E. The 4% fallacy: A methodological and empirical critique of extended care facility population statistics. *Aging and Human Development,* 1973, **4**, 15–22.

Kastenbaum, R., & Durkee, N. Young people view old age. In R. Kastenbaum (Ed.), *New thoughts on old age.* New York: Springer, 1964.

Kinsey, A. C., Pomeroy, W. B., & Martin, C. E. *Sexual behavior in the human male.* Philadelphia: Saunders, 1948.

Kinsey, A. C., Pomeroy, W. B., Martin, C. E., & Gebhard, P. H. *Sexual behavior in the human female.* Philadelphia: Saunders, 1953.

Kogan, N., & Wallach, M. A. Age changes in values and attitudes. *Journal of Gerontology,* 1961, **16,** 272–280.

Kramer, M., Taube, C. A., & Redick, R. W. Patterns of use of psychiatric facilities by the aged: Past, present, and future. In C. Eisdorfer & M. P. Lawton (Eds.), *The psychology of adult development and aging.* Washington, D. C.: American Psychological Association, 1972.

Kramer, M., Taube, C., & Starr, S. Patterns of use of psychiatric facilities by the aged: Current status, trends, and implications. Washington, D.C.: American Psychiatric Association, 1968.

Kuhlen, R. G. Aging and life adjustment. In J. E. Birren (Ed.), *Handbook of aging and the individual.* Chicago: University of Chicago Press, 1959.

Lawton, M. P., & Nahemow, L. Ecology and the aging process. In C. Eisdorfer & M. P. Lawton (Eds.), *The psychology of adult development and aging.* Washington, D. C.: American Psychological Association, 1972.

Leaf, A. Getting old. *Scientific American,* 1973, **229** (Sept.), 45–52.

Lehman, H. C. *Age and achievement.* Princeton: Princeton University Press, 1953.

Lieberman, M. A. The relationship of mortality rates to entrance to a home for the aged. *Geriatrics,* 1961, **16,** 515–519.

Lipman, A. Role conceptions of couples in retirement. In C. Tibbits & W. Donahue (Eds.), *Social and psychological aspects of aging.* New York: Columbia University Press, 1962.

Lipsitt, D. A medical-psychological approach to dependency in the aged. In R. A. Kalish (Ed.), *Dependencies of old people. Occasional Papers in Gerontology,* Volume 6. Ann Arbor and Detroit: Institute of Gerontology, University of Michigan and Wayne State University, 1969.

Lowenthal, M. F. Some potentialities of a life-cycle approach to the study of retirement. In F. M. Carp (Ed.), *Retirement.* New York: Behavioral Publications, 1972.

Lowenthal, M. F., & Haven, C. Interaction and adaptation: Intimacy as a critical variable. *American Sociological Review,* 1968, **33,** 20–30.

MacFarland, R. A. The sensory and perceptual processes in aging. In K. W. Schaie (Ed.), *Theory and methods of research on aging.* Morgantown, West Virginia: West Virginia University Library, 1968.

Maddox, G. Activity and morale: A longitudinal study of selected subjects. *Social Forces,* 1963, **42,** 195–204.

Masters, W. H., & Johnson, V. E. *Human sexual response.* Boston: Little, Brown, 1966.

Masters, W. H., & Johnson, V. E. *Human sexual inadequacy.* Boston: Little, Brown, 1970.

Maxwell, R. J. The changing status of elders in a Polynesian society. *Aging and Human Development,* 1970, **1,** 137–146.

McKain, W. *Retirement marriage.* Storrs, Connecticut: University of Connecticut Press, 1968.

McTavish, D. G. Perceptions of old people: A review of research methodologies and findings. *The Gerontologist,* 1971, **11**(4, Pt. 2), 90–102.

Moberg, D. O. *Spiritual well-being* (White House Conference on Aging background papers). Washington, D. C.: Government Printing Office, 1971.

Moenster, P. A. Learning and memory in relation to age. *Journal of Gerontology,* 1972, **27**, 361–363.

Neugarten, B. L. Adult personality: Toward a psychology of the life cycle. In B. L. Neugarten (Ed.), *Middle age and aging.* Chicago: University of Chicago Press, 1968.

Neugarten, B. L. Personality and the aging process. *The Gerontologist,* 1972, **12,** (Spring, Pt. 1), 9–15.

Neugarten, B. L., Havighurst, R. J., & Tobin, S. S. The measurement of life satisfaction. *Journal of Gerontology,* 1961, **16**, 134–143.

Neugarten, B. L., Havighurst, R. J., & Tobin, S. S. Personality and patterns of aging. In B. L. Neugarten (Ed.), *Middle age and aging.* Chicago: University of Chicago Press, 1968.

Neugarten, B. L., Moore, J. W., & Lowe, J. C. Age norms, age constraints, and adult socialization. *American Journal of Sociology,* 1965, **70**, 710–717.

Neugarten, B. L., & Weinstein, K. K. The changing American grandparent. *Journal of Marriage and the Family,* 1964, **26**, 199–204.

Nimkoff, M. F. Family relationships of older people. *The Gerontologist,* 1961, **1**, 92–97.

Oberleder, M. Psychotherapy with the aging: An art of the possible? *Psychotherapy: Theory, Research, and Practice,* 1966, **3**, 139–142.

Palmore, E. Retirement patterns among aged men: Findings of the 1963 survey of the aged. *Social Security Bulletin,* 1964, **27** (Aug.), 3–10.

Parkes, C. M. "Seeking" and "finding" a lost object: Evidence from recent studies of the reaction to bereavement. *Social Science and Medicine,* 1970, **4**, 187–201.

Parkes, C. M. *Bereavement: Studies of grief in adult life.* New York: International Universities Press, 1972.

Peterson, D. A. Financial adequacy in retirement: Perceptions of older Americans. *The Gerontologist,* 1972, **12**, 379–383.

Pfeiffer, E. Sexual behavior in old age. In E. W. Busse & E. Pfeiffer (Eds.), *Behavior and adaptation in late life.* Boston: Little, Brown, 1969.

Planek, T. W., Condon, M. E., & Fowler, R. C. *An investigation of the problems and opinions of aged drivers.* Chicago, Illinois: National Safety Council, 1968. Cited in Case et al., 1970.

Plutchik, R., Weiner, M., & Conte, H. Studies of body image, body worries, and body discomforts. *Journal of Gerontology,* 1971, **26**, 244–350.

Reichard, S., Livson, F., & Petersen, P. G. *Aging and personality: A study of 87 older men.* New York: Wiley, 1962.

Revis, J. S. *Transportation* (White House Conference on Aging background papers). Washington, D. C.: Government Printing Office, 1971.

Riegel, K. F., & Riegel, R. M. Development, drop and death. *Developmental Psychology,* 1972, **6**, 306–319.

Riley, M. W., Foner, A., & Associates. *Aging and society: Volume I, An inventory of research findings.* New York: Russell Sage, 1968.

Rodstein, M. Accidents among the aged: Incidence, causes, and prevention. *Journal of Chronic Diseases,* 1964, **17**, 515–526.

Rosow, I. *Social integration of the aged.* New York: Free Press, 1967.

Ross, E. K. *On death and dying.* New York: Macmillan, 1969.

Saltz, R. Aging persons as child-care workers in a Foster Grandparent program: Psychosocial effects and work performance. *Aging and Human Development,* 1971, **2**, 314–340.

Schaie, K. W., Labouvie, G. V., & Barrett, T. J. Selective attrition effects in a fourteen-year study of adult intelligence. *Journal of Gerontology,* 1973, **28,** 328–334.

Schaie, K. W., & Strother, C. R. A cross-sectional study of age changes in cognitive behavior. *Psychological Bulletin,* 1968, **70,** 671–680.

Schonfield, D. Learning and retention. In J. E. Birren (Ed.), *Contemporary gerontology: Concepts and issues.* Los Angeles: Andrus Gerontology Center, 1969.

Shanas, E. *The health of older people: A social survey.* Cambridge, Massachusetts: Harvard University Press, 1962.

Shanas, E., Townsend, P., Wedderburn, D., Friis, H., Milhoj, P., & Stehouwer, J. The psychology of health. In B. Neugarten (Ed.), *Middle age and aging.* Chicago: University of Chicago Press, 1968. (a)

Shanas, E., Townsend, P., Wedderburn, D., Friis, H., Milhoj, P., & Stehouwer, J. (Eds.), *Old people in three industrial societies.* New York: Atherton, 1968. (b)

Shelton, A. J. Igbo child-rearing, eldership, and dependence: A comparison of two cultures. In R. A. Kalish (Ed.), *Dependencies of old people.* In *Occasional Papers in Gerontology,* Volume 6. Ann Arbor and Detroit: Institute of Gerontology, University of Michigan and Wayne State University, 1969.

Sherman, E. M., & Brittan, M. R. Contemporary food gatherers. *The Gerontologist,* 1973, **13** (3, Pt. 1), 358–364.

Silverman, P. R. Widowhood and preventive intervention. *The Family Coordinator,* 1972, **21,** 95–102.

Simmons, L. W. *The role of the aged in primitive society.* New Haven: Yale University Press, 1945.

Simon, A. *Mental health.* In *Physical and Mental Health* (White House Conference on Aging background papers). Washington, D. C.: Government Printing Office, 1971.

Smith, H. E. Family interaction patterns of the aged: A review. In A. M. Rose & W. A. Peterson (Eds.), *Older people and their social world.* Philadelphia: F. A. Davis, 1965.

Spieth, W. Cardiovascular health status, age, and psychological performance. *Journal of Gerontology,* 1964, **19,** 277–284.

Streib, G. F. Family patterns in retirement. *Journal of Social Issues,* 1958, **14**(2), 46–60.

Streib, G. F. Are the aged a minority group? In A. W. Gouldner & S. M. Miller (Eds.), *Applied sociology.* New York: Free Press, 1965. Republished in Neugarten, B. L. (Ed.), *Middle age and aging.* Chicago: University of Chicago Press, 1968.

Streib, G. F., & Thompson, W. E. Situational determinants: Health and economic deprivation in retirement. *Journal of Social Issues,* 1958, **14**(2), 18–34.

Sussman, M. B. The help pattern in the middle-class family. *American Sociological Review,* 1953, **18,** 22–28.

Sussman, M. B. Relationships of adult children with their parents in the United States. In E. Shanas & G. Streib (Eds.), *Social structure and the family: Generational relations.* Englewood Cliffs, New Jersey: Prentice-Hall, 1965.

Szafran, J., & Birren, J. E. Perception. In J. E. Birren (Ed.), *Contemporary gerontology: Concepts and issues.* Los Angeles: Andrus Gerontology Center, 1969.

Taub, H. A., & Long, M. K. The effects of practice on short-term memory of young and old subjects. *Journal of Gerontology,* 1972, **27,** 494–499.

Troll, L. E. The family of later life: A decade review. *Journal of Marriage and the Family,* 1971, **33,** 263–290.

USDHEW, National Institute for Neurological Diseases and Blindness. *Annual tabulations of the model reporting area for blindness statistics, 1965, statistical report.* Washington, D. C.: Government Printing Office, 1966.

USDHEW. *Working with older people: A guide to practice. Volume II: Biological, psychological, and sociological aspects of aging.* Washington, D. C.: Public Health Service, 1970.

USDHEW. *Health in the later years of life: Selected data from the National Center for Health Statistics.* Washington, D. C.: Government Printing Office, 1971.

Veroff, J. The use of thematic aperception to assess motivation in a nationwide interview study. *Psychological Monographs,* 1960, **74,** 1–32.

Weisman, A. *On dying and denying.* New York: Behavioral Publications, 1972.

White House Conference on Aging. *Aging and blindness, Special Concerns Session report.* Washington, D. C.: Government Printing Office, 1972.

Wolff, K. *Geriatric psychiatry.* Springfield, Illinois: C. C. Thomas, 1963.

Author Index

Subject Index